Prarambh

Transition from Campus to Corporate

Dr. Jimmy Jain

Accolades for the Book

"Prarambh: Transition from Campus to Corporate" has very useful knowledge about corporate. Excellent content and useful.

Manoj Aggarwal
Group Associate Vice President and Head, DCB Bank, Mumbai

"Prarambh: Transition from Campus to Corporate" is Simple. Specific. Easy to Learn. An excellent read for everyone.

Shashi Bhatia
Learning and Development, Royal Enfield, Mumbai

This book is like a foundation for anyone who want to showcase as someone who is capable and accountable. A must have guide - with practical tips for managing the transition into a corporate or solopreneur journey.

Deepa Kaur Padda
Founder, Burgeon Skills, Mumbai

"Prarambh - Transition from Campus to Corporate" by Jimmy Jain is an insightful and practical guide for students transitioning from academic life to the professional world. Drawing from his own experiences as a management trainee, entrepreneur and sales trainer, Jimmy provides readers with invaluable advice and strategies to navigate the early stages of their careers. This book can really be a game-changer! The strategy can actually help an individual transform their mindset, personality and other attributes at work and personal life both. I'm sure after reading the concepts and applying the same in daily life can bring drastic change in one's life. I'm looking forward to use most of the methods described in my work-life.

Megha Jain
Wealth Manager,
ICICI Prudential AMC, Mumbai

When we study a professional course, we create an idea and a picture of the corporate world in our mind. When we arrive in corporate corridors, we find that there is quite a difference. Then we try to adept and adopt to the situation. This at times takes lots of time. This book can be an ideal one for the new entrants for their transition period. This book can make them more employable and give them a good start to their careers. Its right been named as Prarambh. Congratulations to Dr. Jimmy Jain to come up with a book on such a relevant topic.

Arvind Mishra

Director Sales Solutions,

Square Sequel Consulting Pvt Ltd., Mumbai

The book is industry-neutral, making it relevant for individuals across various fields. Jimmy's writing is clear, engaging, and filled with real-world scenarios that bring his concepts to life. He effectively addresses common challenges faced by newcomers in the corporate world and offers actionable solutions.

One of the book's standout features is its emphasis on grooming, verbal & written communication, continuous learning and skill acquisition. Knowing Jimmy, who started his carrier as frontline sales officer & transitioned to a capability building coach & then a design thinking professional, draws lessons from his own journey & narrates about importance of upgrading capabilities that serves as a powerful example for readers. His passion for personal and professional growth is evident throughout the book, inspiring readers to invest in their development. The book also delves into the nuances of corporate culture, communication, and professional behavior, providing readers with a comprehensive understanding of what is expected in a professional setting. Jimmy's insights into networking, building relationships, conflict management and leveraging opportunities are particularly valuable for those at the beginning of their careers.

To summarise, "Prarambh - Transition from Campus to Corporate" is a must-read for students and young professionals. Jimmy Jain's experience and expertise shine through, making this book a practical and motivational resource for anyone looking to succeed in the corporate world. Whether you are just starting your career or seeking to enhance your professional skills, this book offers the guidance and inspiration needed to thrive.

Bharatendu Kapoor
President - Sales and Marketing,
Tractors and Farm Equipment Ltd, Chennai

Transitioning from the academic world into the professional sphere is a significant milestone in anyone's life. It is a journey that can be both exciting and daunting, filled with opportunities and challenges that require a new set of skills and attitudes. The shift from the structured environment of school or university to the dynamic and often unpredictable world of work demands more than just technical knowledge—it requires an understanding of professional behaviour, effective communication, and a positive mental outlook.

This book is an essential guide for anyone preparing to make this important transition. Jimmy draws on his extensive experience in the academic and business worlds to provide you with a roadmap for success and practical tools, covering a wide range of topics that are crucial for thriving in a professional setting.

You will find clear and concise advice on how to present yourself professionally, from writing effective emails to developing a confident personal style. Jimmy emphasises traits that are highly valued in any workplace.

As you embark on this new chapter of your life, let this book be your guide. Embrace the practical advice it offers, and you will find yourself well-prepared to face the challenges and seize the opportunities that lie ahead. This is more than just a guidebook; it is a companion for your journey into the professional world, providing the support and wisdom you need to succeed.

Katie Lewis

COO, Co-Founder, Aspire, London

Jimmy's new book serves as a valuable guide for recent graduates and budding professionals entering the corporate world. With genuine intent, he aims to be the first coach for those transitioning from academia to their professional careers.

At first glance, some of the topics might seem obvious to seasoned professionals. I, too, felt this way initially. However, reflecting on my own journey 18 years ago, I realized that these basics were exactly what I struggled with, often seeking genuine advice on these very subjects.

These are the kinds of topics that frequently come up during performance reviews and one-on-one feedback sessions. In the corporate world, understanding the right behaviors (the "how") is just as crucial as possessing functional knowledge (the "why").

Jimmy's book is an essential reference for any new professional in their early days of settling into the corporate environment. Kudos to Jimmy for bringing such a helpful resource to the youth, and thank you for your contribution.

Deepak Mishra

Senior General Manager, CP Milk and Food Products,

Lucknow

If one asks, what will I tell to the 23 year old me who graduated out of business school that time - " Read this book "

This kind of guidance is required to everyone who is taking that big step of completing education and starting their professional journey. The words and practical tips on of professionalism given in the book are very achievable, can be practiced without much effort and it's almost like a ready reckoner which can be checked every day.

Definition of Communication skills, body language and especially the impact of power dressing (Power dressing goes beyond attire!!) cover the key aspects of how a person should be in terms of physical presence, Verbal presence and portray the right behaviour every Young professional needs it on Day Zero.

Active Listening, Nonverbal communication, Empathy are key factors for the senior leaders, and if one masters them during the journey from Day One it would be a successful journey and more importantly will be inspiring to many .

The importance of Values which should be the DNA of every professional which makes or breaks a person has been emphasised with great examples and tips to learn. World is never alone and Corporate world is all about relationships and active interaction with numerous roles and hence people skills like reading people, interpersonal skills, managing Conflict have been explained and the secrets of all his (Jimmy's) experience has been shared in this book.

One word to say to Jimmy on this - Where were you when I started my career Jimmy?

Pavan Valluri
Vice President – Consulting, CGI, Bangalore

To my parents,

who constantly guide me and keep me sane.

To my wife,

who supports, tolerates, and accepts me

as

I am.

To my daughter, Lovicca.

This book is dedicated to the dynamic and ambitious young professionals worldwide who stand at the threshold of entering the corporate realm.

To aspiring talents across the globe, it's a nod to the transition where the ink of knowledge meets the canvas of professional possibilities. It recognizes your commitment, enthusiasm, and readiness to contribute to the professional world.

Young professionals, this is your formal acknowledgement—a step towards the challenges, triumphs, and growth that await you. Consider this dedication a symbolic handshake as you step into the realm of corporate excellence.

More power to each one of you! This dedication is a mark of respect for your dedication and a recognition of the immense potential you bring to the professional arena. Here's to your success and the impactful contributions you are poised to make.

What I do is my Dharma
(My duty, my responsibility).
What others do is their Karma
(Their actions).

All the proceeds from this book

Will support the charitable initiative

sponsored by

Square Sequel Consulting Private Limited.

Foreword By Manish Ghaneckar

In the day and age of generative AI, robotic assistance and augmented reality, modern workplaces are becoming increasingly hybrid, automated and remote. Gone are the days when technical expertise alone ensured success. Success today demands not only consistent and unwavering professionalism but also effective communication, tailored to the complexities of a fast-changing world.

As a Leadership Coach, I have witnessed first-hand the transformative power of embracing professionalism. An embodiment of integrity, clarity of values, and a positive mindset brings together an aura that conveys control, poise and confidence. Having mentored many diverse individuals, I have shared one common recommendation for them – that it's never too late to begin working on oneself, though earlier the better.

The chapters within this book provide invaluable insights into understanding and building a professional image, mastering clarity in written and verbal elucidation, and using the subtle art of body language. Each section is designed to equip young professionals with the tools needed to become eloquent communicators, foster strong interpersonal relationships, manage conflict effectively, and make informed decisions.

One of the most profound lessons in this book is the emphasis on aligning personal values with professional actions. By doing so and from early on in their careers, individuals can achieve a sense of fulfilment and authenticity that resonates throughout their careers, helps seal trust and makes good leaders. Effective tips to cultivate incremental habits, the significance of teamwork, and the impact of a positive mental attitude are explored in depth, highlighting how these elements contribute to foundational success and rapid personal growth.

Whether one is starting a career journey or looking to refine their professional demeanor, this book encourages continuous learning, self-awareness, and a commitment to excellence—qualities that are essential for any aspiring leader.

A blend of timeless wisdom and practical advice, this book equips the reader with a comprehensive guide to navigate the complexities of the modern workplace.

In a chaotic world mired by too much screen time and diminishing attention spans, the principles outlined in this book remain steadfast and evergreen in their ability to help young professionals make solid impact and leave an indelible impression. They serve as a beacon for those striving to not only achieve professional excellence but also to inspire and lead others with integrity and empathy.

I am confident that the insights and strategies presented here will empower the reader to prioritize professional finesse, clear dialogue and value-based living.

Manish Ghaneckar

CEO and Executive Coach, Global Conceptss

www.manishghaneckar.com

Foreword By
Anil Santhapuri

As we stand on the brink of the Fourth Industrial Revolution, a wave of technological advancements is reshaping industries and lives. India, with its demographic advantage and rich skill set, is poised to become a $10 trillion economy by 2030. It is crucial that we equip our youth with the skills and mindset necessary to spearhead this Industry 4.0 revolution.

While this presents a significant opportunity for our nation and its youth, it's important to acknowledge the realities that accompany it. I will introduce three perspectives to shed light on this - the Leadership Pipeline framework, my personal experience, and insights from the World Economic Forum.

Ram Charan, a renowned author and CEO advisor, discusses in his work the Leadership Pipeline and the six transitions an employee must make to ascend from an individual contributor to a CEO. This assumes that a first-time job holder possesses all the necessary skills to make a successful "Campus to Corporate" transition (let's call this the "zeroth" transition). This "employability challenge" is particularly significant in India, where the readiness of a new graduate to take on a job is often lacking, especially in terms of behavioral skills.

Having joined the corporate world in 2002, I have spent the last 15 years working as an HR, Talent, and Learning professional. Despite our annual efforts to facilitate the "Campus to Corporate" transition for new graduates, achieving complete employability readiness remains a distant dream, more so getting a 100% employable graduate straight of a Campus. The need for this transition is more critical now than ever.

The World Economic Forum's Future of Jobs report highlights the Top 10 Skills of 2025, with a majority focused around problem-solving, self-management, and interpersonal collaboration. However, there is a gap between these future job skills and what is currently taught in our universities and colleges.

These perspectives lead me to conclude that the "Campus to Corporate" transition, or the "zeroth" career transition as I have coined it, requires both a change in mindset and skillset. We must be deliberate and intentional about this transition.

This is where "Prarambh" by Dr. Jimmy Jain comes in. It is a commendable effort to enable our youth to take charge of their "Campus to Corporate" transition. This book will serve as a valuable resource for today's youth aspiring to make a successful career start, focusing on themes such as self-management, interpersonal skills, communication, and other relevant mindset and skills. It will also be a great resource for organizations and their Learning departments to enhance their Campus to Corporate programs.

In the spirit of role qualification, I envision a future where resources like this are used in universities and colleges to prepare students to be "employability-ready" even before they join corporates. Most importantly, it encourages the youth to take full ownership of their career aspirations and make a successful first and critical step.

Here's to better career beginnings with "Prarambh."

Anil Santhapuri

Head – Academy for Management and Leadership Excellence

TVS Motor Company

Contents

Contents

Acknowledgements

I have many people to acknowledge and express my gratitude. People who believed in me, my readers, my audience, my participants, and my clients who continue to put their faith and trust in my services and give me the opportunities to make a difference in the lives of people I come in contact with, in the process make me live my passion.

The unending support of my family, Mrs. Bimla Jain my mom, Sh. Gian Sagar Jain my dad, my wife Usha, and my daughter Lovicca. I just can't thank them enough.

My team at my workplace believes in me, helps me put my ideas into action, and commits their time, energy, and efforts to make our workplace a place to have fun and learn. I want to thank my inner circle of Ms. Zoya Natterwala, Mr. Randheer K. Mall, and the editor of this book, Ms. Afreen Fatima.

This book would not have been possible without all of you. You give me tremendous thirst in my journey. To act as a catalyst in people's lives, I am blessed to live my dreams, and I have an amazing life. I pray to God almighty to give me the strength and power to continue supporting people to unlock their innate potential and live the life of their dreams.

List of people who have had an impact on my life thus far (in alphabetical order)

Sr	Name
1	Shri. Acharya Gopal Dutt Sharma
2	Capt. Kanu Pathania
3	Dr. A.H. Kalro
4	Dr. Anandakuttan B Unnithan
5	Dr. Ashish Phadnis
6	Dr. Hitu Mahajan
7	Dr. Krishnamurthy Iyer
8	Dr. Shaji Gopinath
9	Dr. Srini Pillay
10	Dr. Swati Sarangi
11	Late Mr. Nelson Mandela
12	Late Sh. Gautam Nagwekar
13	Late Sh. Venkat Subramanian Thyagarajan

Sr	Name
14	Mr. Abhijit Shah
15	Mr. Ajit Issac
16	Mr. Aman Sodhi
17	Mr. Anand Mahindra
18	Mr. Anil Chhikara
19	Mr. Anil Santhapuri
20	Mr. Arvind Mishra
21	Mr. Arsen Harutyunyan
22	Mr. Baharatendu Kapoor
23	Mr. Bharat Dhruv
24	Mr. Bharatendu Kapoor
25	Mr. Binoj Vasu
26	Mr. Dinesh Laungani
27	Mr. Dipankar Paul
28	Mr. Elvis Colaco
29	Mr. G.S.Gill
30	Mr. Gaurav Arora
31	Mr. Gaurav Sharma
32	Mr. Hakob Hakobyan

Sr	Name
33	Mr. Hemant Shetty
34	Mr. Jitendra More
35	Mr. Joseph Reddy Salibindla
36	Mr. K. Ravi
37	Mr. Kapil Dev
38	Mr. Kapil Premchandani
39	Mr. Kaushal Parikh
40	Mr. Leander Peas
41	Mr. Manish Ghaneckar
42	Mr. Manjith Mohan
43	Mr. N. C. Suresh
44	Mr. N. Ranganath
45	Mr. Neeraj Saroj
46	Mr. Nikhil Bhende
47	Mr. PHR Virendra
48	Mr. Prakash Anthony
49	Mr. Prasad Salunke
50	Mr. R. S. Deshpande
51	Mr. Rajesh Fanda

Sr	Name
52	Mr. Ranjan Gupta
53	Mr. Ritesh Ranjan
54	Mr. Robin Sharma
55	Mr. Roger Federer
56	Mr. Sameer Sortur
57	Mr. Sankha Bhowmick
58	Mr. Satish Sapru
59	Ms. Shivani Jain
60	Mr. Suntosh Punganur
61	Mr. Tigran Petrosyan
62	Mr. Tushar Vaidya
63	Mr. Vinod Shetty
64	Mr. Vipul Chheda
65	Mr. Yadhu Kishore Nandikolla
66	Mrs. Joginder Grewal
67	Ms. Archana Karfa
68	Ms. Arundhati Chafekar
69	Ms. Clara D'Silva
70	Ms. Deepa Kaur

Sr	Name
71	Ms. Deepa Vishwanathan
72	Ms. Deepika Padukone
73	Ms. Jyoti Tiwari
74	Ms. Katie Lewis
75	Ms. Ketki Ghatge
76	Ms. Kusum Prasad
77	Ms. Lakshmi Sreenivasan
78	Ms. Monika Mangla
79	Ms. Neelanjana Saxena
80	Ms. Pooja Rai
81	Ms. Priti Irani
82	Ms. Priya Pathak
83	Ms. Puja Biyani
84	Ms. Rachna Taranath
85	Ms. Rita Daniel
86	Ms. Sonali Desai
87	Ms. Tejashree Abhishek
88	Ms. Zaruhi Shushanyan

How to Use this Book?

Congratulations on taking the first step towards transforming your life from campus to corporate! This guidebook is your roadmap to crafting an exceptional life as you transition into the professional world. Designed with careful consideration, this book offers a comprehensive approach to help you design the life you've always envisioned.

As you navigate this book, remember that your journey from campus to corporate is uniquely yours. Each chapter is designed to empower you with the tools you need, offering guidance while respecting your individuality and aspirations. Whether you're reading cover to cover or focusing on specific topics, this book is your constant companion on your transformative journey.

By the time you finish reading, you'll have gained a fresh perspective on the professional front and a newfound sense of purpose. You will enter your workplace with a new perspective, and the world around you will be transformed, setting the stage for a brighter tomorrow.

If you find yourself seeking guidance or clarification during your journey, don't hesitate to reach out to me at jimmy@jimmyjain.com. Your success is my priority, and I am here to support you every step of the way.

Here's to your transformational journey from campus to corporate and the exceptional life that awaits you!

Cheers to ongoing learning and growth!

Dr. Jimmy Jain

jimmy@jimmyjain.com

Prologue

In the pages that follow, you're about to embark on a transformative journey – a journey that spans the chasm between the sheltered world of academia and the fast-paced realm of corporate professionalism. This book, "Campus to Corporate," is more than just a guide; it's your trusted companion as you transition from the campus life to the corporate life.

The intention behind crafting this book was simple yet profound: to bridge the gap between the theoretical knowledge you've acquired in lecture halls and the practical skills demanded by the corporate landscape. As you stand at the precipice of this significant shift, it's only natural to feel a mix of excitement and trepidation. You might wonder, "How do I navigate this new environment? How do I excel in my career? How do I ensure that I stand out among the multitude of professionals out there?"

These are precisely the questions we aim to address. From the initial steps of crafting your professional identity to the intricate art of networking, from mastering the nuances of effective communication to fostering continuous learning, each chapter of this book is designed to provide you with actionable insights, practical tips, and real-world examples that illuminate your path.

Your journey from campus to corporate is not just a transition; it's a transformation – a transformation that goes beyond acquiring skills to becoming a confident, adaptable, and resourceful professional. This book is your compass, guiding you through the uncharted waters of corporate life and helping you navigate the challenges and seize the opportunities that lie ahead.

These topics are the ones I use in my workshops while conducting Campus to Corporate transitioning sessions. But remember, this book isn't just for those fresh out of college. Its wisdom and practical advice can be a valuable resource at any stage of your career. Whether you're just starting out or seeking to rejuvenate your professional journey, you'll find insights that resonate.

You can pick any chapter and begin from anywhere. Like a well-planned journey, the flexibility to chart your own course is yours. As you flip through these pages, envision yourself as an eager learner, an enthusiastic contributor, and a proactive individual who's ready to embrace the new experiences that await. Remember, this book is more than a guide – it's a roadmap to unlocking your full potential in the corporate world.

So let us embark on this journey together and uncover the strategies, insights, and wisdom that will empower you to make the most of your transition.

Etiquette
Empowers
Excellence

Chapter 1

Introduction to Professionalism

Vaibhav had recently graduated from college and had several interviews lined up. Though he excelled in academics, he was hesitant about navigating the uncharted trails of the corporate world. Despite his excellent training and learning experiences in college, he was anxious about transitioning to the new corporate climate. In school and college, there were fixed junctures for moving from one class to the next, but now uncertainty was setting in, and he wasn't sure of his first step.

As he searched for inspiration from different sources, he suddenly remembered his uncle, Sivaranjan, a Vice President at a major corporation. Sivaranjan had once told Vaibhav to reach out whenever needed. Vaibhav quickly dialled his uncle's number.

"Uncle, I need your guidance," Vaibhav began, pouring his heart out about his challenges and sense of direction.

Sivaranjan listened patiently. "Vaibhav, why don't we meet up and discuss this in detail?"

They decided to meet at 11:30 am on a Saturday morning at Sivaranjan's home. Vaibhav reached with a list of questions in hand. They chatted for a bit, and then Vaibhav kickstarted the conversation by asking, "Uncle, what's the first step to land in the uncertain corporate world?"

Sivaranjan smiled. "Vaibhav, there's a Seminar on Managing and Nurturing Talent coming up, where I am invited as the keynote speaker. It's an excellent opportunity for you to gain insights into the corporate world. There will be a talk on transitioning from campus to corporate that I think you'll find particularly beneficial. Why don't you join me there?"

A few days later, Vaibhav attended the seminar. The event was bustling with energy, filled with aspiring professionals and seasoned industry veterans. Vaibhav felt a mix of excitement and nervousness as he took his seat among the audience.

Sivaranjan took the stage, delivering a compelling keynote speech on professionalism and effective communication in the corporate world. Vaibhav listened intently, taking notes and absorbing every word.

After finishing his talk, Sivaranjan stepped down from the podium and mingled with the audience. Vaibhav followed closely, eager to see his uncle in action. Sivaranjan noticed a familiar face approaching him as they chatted with various attendees. It was Mr. Sharma, an old friend and colleague.

"Siva, that was an excellent talk," Mr. Sharma said, shaking his hand warmly.

"Thank you, Sharma. It's always a pleasure to share my experiences," Sivaranjan replied.

As they caught up, Mr. Sharma mentioned his daughter. "Siva, I've been meaning to talk to you about Ananya. She's just graduated and is about to start her first job. She's in that critical transition phase from academic life to the corporate world. I think she could benefit from some guidance."

Sivaranjan considered this for a moment. "You know, I'm already mentoring my nephew, Vaibhav. I think it would be great to have Ananya join us. ***Mentorship can make a big difference, and having different perspectives will enrich the experience for everyone.***"

The following weekend, Sivaranjan arranged a meeting at his office for both Vaibhav and Ananya to kick off their mentorship journey. Vaibhav arrived first, and shortly after, Ananya joined them.

Sivaranjan looked at both of them from top to bottom and gave a smirk. Vaibhav had shown up in loafers and a stubble, looking like he had just rolled out of bed, while Ananya walked in wearing rugged jeans and a casual top. He gestured for them to sit.

"Vaibhav, this is Ananya," Sivaranjan introduced. "Ananya, meet Vaibhav, my nephew. He's also entering the corporate world soon."

Vaibhav extended his hand. "Hi Ananya, nice to meet you."

Ananya shook his hand, smiling. "Hi Vaibhav, nice to meet you too. I'm looking forward to learning together."

"I'm glad you both could make it. The corporate world can be challenging, however, with the right guidance, you can navigate it successfully. Let's start by discussing what you both hope to gain from this mentorship."

Vaibhav spoke first. "Uncle, I want to understand the unwritten rules of corporate culture, how to communicate effectively, and how to make a good first impression. I've realized that the professional world operates on a different set of norms and expectations, and I want to be prepared to meet those head-on."

Ananya nodded. "I feel the same, Uncle. I'm also interested in learning how to build strong professional relationships. But beyond that, I want to understand how to maintain a balance between work and life. I've heard that managing your image and relationships at work is crucial, and I don't want to make any missteps early in my career."

Sivaranjan smiled, pleased with their enthusiasm. "Those are all excellent goals. We'll cover various topics over our sessions, starting with the basics of professionalism. Remember, your journey is unique, and your growth will depend on your willingness to learn and adapt."

Ananya leaned forward, her eyes shining with determination. "I'm ready to learn, Uncle. I know there's a lot I need to work on, but I'm committed."

Vaibhav nodded in agreement. "Me too, Uncle. I'm ready to put in the effort."

"Great," Sivaranjan leaned forward and said, "You will learn a lot about the professional world. ***This world will shout out what it is, and nobody will walk you through the concepts of what it is not.*** Let's start by discussing the misconceptions or myths about the professional world or professionalism."

Myths About Professionalism
Pay check

"Does earning good money make a person professional?" Vaibhav asked.

Sivaranjan shook his head. "Some people think the higher the salary, the higher the professionalism. They measure professionalism based on how fat the pay check is. Is it justifiable to base professionalism on the number of zeroes on the pay check and then keep blabbering around like real immatures in the workplace?"

Ananya added, "I've seen that mindset among my friends too. They believe that once they land a high-paying job, they're automatically professionals. It's a common misconception."

Vaibhav nodded, starting to see the distinction.

Credentials

"It is commonly believed that possessing a degree automatically qualifies someone as a professional," Sivaranjan continued. "But simply having a degree does not guarantee professionalism. While formal education is undoubtedly valuable and often a prerequisite for a professional journey, true professionalism extends beyond academic qualifications. It encompasses qualities such as integrity, reliability, ethical conduct, effective communication, and a commitment to continuous learning and improvement."

"So, it's more about how you conduct yourself rather than just your qualifications?" Vaibhav asked.

"Exactly," Sivaranjan affirmed. "These attributes, combined with relevant skills and experience, truly define a professional in any field."

Ananya nodded thoughtfully.

Sivaranjan leaned back, allowing Vaibhav and Ananya to absorb the insights. "Now that we've debunked some common myths, let's delve deeper into understanding what true professionalism entails."

What is Professionalism?

"Professionalism is defined as someone's behavior, conduct, and attitude in a work or business environment," Sivaranjan explained. "Regardless of any specific profession, a person should demonstrate important qualities and characteristics of a professional. Professionalism leads to workplace success, a solid reputation, and a strong work ethic and level of excellence."

Vaibhav recalled a study he had read. "Is it true that employers who hire college graduates consider professionalism and work ethic as essential competencies?"

"Absolutely," Sivaranjan replied. "In fact, 97.5% of employers identify it as essential for the success of a new college hire."

In his book, *True Professionalism*, David H. Maister, a former Harvard Business School professor, says that **'professionalism is not a label you give yourself—**

it's a description you hope others will apply to you.'

As Vaibhav nodded in agreement with Sivaranjan's insights, he felt a newfound appreciation for the importance of professionalism in his upcoming career endeavors. "Understanding that professionalism is not just about qualifications but about how we conduct ourselves is crucial," he remarked, eager to explore further how this principle shapes the corporate landscape.

Ananya added, "I agree. In college, we had workshops on professionalism, however, they mostly focused on resumes and interviews. It's eye-opening to realize that true professionalism is about our daily actions and attitudes."

With their discussion on the essence of professionalism resonating deeply, Vaibhav, Ananya, and Sivaranjan were now poised to explore the impact of it in the corporate world, delving into the eminent role professionalism plays in shaping successful careers and fostering organizational excellence.

The Eminence of Professionalism

"Professionalism at work is crucial and is an essential element for a successful career," Sivaranjan continued. "Organizations emphasize the importance of professionalism because long-term relationships and fruitful interactions with customers or clients contribute to the achievement of company objectives and goals."

"So, professionalism is also about contributing to the company's success?" Vaibhav asked.

"Yes," Sivaranjan nodded. "Managers who exhibit professionalism set appropriate examples of work ethics and workplace conduct for their co-workers and employees."

Ananya chimed in, "It sounds like professionalism is about setting the right example and building strong relationships."

Factors to Highlight the Need for Professionalism in Life and Work

"Let me highlight some key factors that emphasize the need for professionalism," Sivaranjan said.

Encourages Personal Development

"Professional development is all about getting new experiences and learning new skills. Personal development, on the other hand, is the process of assessing those skills and knowledge and using them to set life goals as well as maximize your potential. Professionalism goes side by side with enhancing professional development and personal growth. Furthermore, professional work environments promote professional behavior and appropriate workplace conduct."

Enhances Respect

Taking the high road isn't always easy, especially when someone else misbehaves or crosses a line. Professionalism serves as a reminder of how to keep your personal feelings separate from your professional behavior. Professionalism at work fosters respect for even those who are disrespectful.

Ananya shared, "I've learned that maintaining professionalism, even in challenging situations, can earn you respect and help maintain a positive work environment."

Establishes Appropriate Boundaries

"It is critical to establish appropriate workplace boundaries. Professionalism at work aids in the separation of business and personal lives. Professionalism emphasizes what is considered appropriate workplace behavior and what is not. Employees who behave professionally will be able to avoid crossing boundaries in interactions or conversations with co-workers."

Accountability

"Professionalism aids in the introduction and maintenance of accountability in the workplace. For example, if you send an email in addition to verbal confirmation of a project, you are assuming responsibility for it. This will demonstrate your dedication to the project, its objectives, and deadlines. This will also aid in the establishment of trust with your client or customers."

Vaibhav reflected, "In college, I noticed that group projects went smoother when everyone took responsibility for their parts and communicated clearly. It wasn't just about finishing the project, but about building trust and respect within the team."

Ananya added, "And when there were clear boundaries and respect for each other's time and efforts, the collaboration was much more productive. I can see how these principles are even more critical in a professional setting."

"If you haven't already established strong working relationships that can be relied on to last and deliver results when needed, now is the time to do so. According to research, your ability to empathize with, connect with, and influence others is a critical skill for success. It is critical to be aware of the beliefs, biases, and mindsets that may influence our behavior. It is also critical to cultivate relational maturity that reflects our values and supports our vision. We have to think and behave rationally to sustain any progress we make," Sivaranjan advised.

Attributes of Professionalism

"Professionalism demonstrates that there is more to work than simply meeting targets. It aids in the development of a plan for continuous improvement. You can discover the advantages of working ethically and treating everyone with respect in the workplace," said Sivaranjan.

Maintain A Professional Image

"Having a professional presence at work is a good way to demonstrate your professionalism. In other words, it helps if you dress and groom properly and arrive on time. Employees are the image of a company. It's a good idea to dress appropriately. Client meetings are excellent examples of occasions to dress to impress," Sivaranjan explained.

Ananya remembered, "During our final presentations, those who dressed professionally and were punctual made a stronger impression. It showed that they took their work seriously and respected the audience's time."

Maintain Effective Work Habits

"You have to make it a habit to excel at professionalism. *When you show professionalism in your work, you are better able to prioritize goals and plan and*

manage projects. Follow up with your team manager or leaders to receive feedback and track your progress effectively."

Vaibhav added, "Consistent professional behavior helps in managing tasks efficiently and achieving goals systematically."

Show Integrity

"Everyone makes mistakes at work. However, admitting your error and holding yourself accountable is a core characteristic of professionalism. You demonstrate integrity and emotional maturity by accepting responsibility for your actions. Workplaces value those who are willing to address, accept, and work on their mistakes."

Manage Your Time

"You have to be careful about making the best use of your time, or you will miss deadlines and tasks. Prioritization and planning goals are part of a professional attitude. When you set priorities at work, you can meet your deadlines more efficiently."

Communicate Effectively

"Effective communication is often referred to as the 'bridge between confusion and clarity.' It is a beneficial exercise for improving communication skills. Whether it's online or in person, keep practicing and developing effective communication skills. Allow your words to impact your audience and convey your thoughts in a well-structured and compelling manner."

Develop Self-Awareness

"Being able to manage your emotions is one of the primary signs of professionalism. Learning how to develop self-awareness can assist you in identifying emotional triggers and better managing your reactions. Furthermore, when you receive feedback, learn how to recognize and apply the information. This will help both your personal and professional development."

Ananya said, "It's clear that professionalism isn't just about how others see us, but also about how we see and conduct ourselves. By continuously improving these attributes, we can build successful and fulfilling careers."

Vaibhav agreed, "Yes, and understanding these principles now will give us a solid foundation as we move into our professional lives."

Ways to Exhibit Professionalism at Work

"Here are some practical tips, Vaibhav," Sivaranjan continued. "Be an active and attentive listener, ask questions when necessary, and observe tiny details."

"Got it," Vaibhav said, taking notes. "In college, I noticed that if I was attentive in lectures and asked thoughtful questions, I always seemed more engaged and performed better in group projects."

"Keep upgrading and developing your knowledge and skills. Always be prepared to experience a flare of changing industry standards," Sivaranjan advised. "Punctuality is a proven way to showcase one's professional attitude."

Ananya added, "I remember how important it was to stay updated with the latest research in our field. If I missed a class or didn't keep up with readings, it was easy to fall behind."

"And how about handling information?" Vaibhav asked.

"It is always appreciated when information is available in an organized way, whether you work from the office or home," Sivaranjan replied. "Also, it's quintessential to have good email and phone etiquette. Speaking respectfully over the phone is one way of effective communication."

Ananya nodded, "In college, organizing our research and notes was crucial for writing papers and preparing for exams. And sending clear, polite emails to professors and classmates made a big difference in getting the help and responses we needed."

"That's a lot to remember, uncle," Vaibhav said, smiling.

"Professionalism isn't always a trait that some people have and others don't," Sivaranjan reassured. "Professionalism a cultivated skill, and we can master the art of being professional by adopting these characteristics."

"I'll strive for excellence and exceed expectations, uncle," Vaibhav promised.

"That's the spirit, Vaibhav," Sivaranjan said, smiling warmly. "While you're soaking in all this information about professionalism, remember that it's about continuous learning and improvement."

Ananya chimed in, "In college, we had to constantly adapt to new professors, new subjects, and new ways of learning. That experience taught us that continuous improvement and adaptability are key to success, both academically and professionally."

Vaibhav agreed, "Exactly. And now, applying these lessons to the workplace will help us not only fit in but also stand out in our careers."

Sivaranjan concluded, "Professionalism is a journey, not a destination. Keep learning, keep improving, and you'll find that success follows naturally."

Chapter 2

Effective Communication Skills

"Uncle, I am learning what professionalism is under your guidance, and I see it as a conscious effort to be applied daily in every activity, in every task I do. It is something to develop as a skill that I carry throughout my day," said Vaibhav fervently.

Sivaranjan nodded. "It's great to see your enthusiasm, Vaibhav. Now, let's move to the next level."

"Now, do you know what holds the fort together in any organization? What is that pivotal aspect that contributes to the success of the business?" asked Sivaranjan.

Vaibhav thought for a moment, then shook his head. "I'm not sure, Uncle."

"Is it teamwork or collaboration?" Ananya chimed in, curious to know if she was on the right track. "

Sivaranjan smiled at Ananya's keen interest. "That's a very insightful guess, Ananya," he said, nodding appreciatively. "Teamwork and collaboration are indeed crucial, but there's an even more fundamental aspect that ties everything together."

He paused for a moment to let the anticipation build, then continued, ***"According to a study, companies with highly effective practices enjoy 47% higher total returns to shareholders compared to organizations with poor practices.*** It drives organizations to have the courage to talk about what employees want to hear, redefine the employment deal with changing business conditions, and imbibe the discipline to plan and measure their progress effectively."

"Uncle, I am curious to know about this crucial factor, the key to unlocking the avenue of my corporate journey," asked Vaibhav in anticipation and Ananya's curiosity piqued too.

Sivaranjan took a sip of his coffee, laid back in his chair, and asked, "Tell me, what is keeping you glued to this conversation, apart from wanting to start right from the word go."

Vaibhav gave it a little thought and answered, "The way you are explaining the concepts with interesting facts and questions at the same time."

Ananya said, "For me, Uncle, it's also the way you're relating these concepts to real-world scenarios. It makes everything feel more practical and less abstract, which is really helpful."

"Okay," said Sivaranjan. "Only if I walked you through the process and left out the interesting part, would you be intrigued with the information? No!"

Vaibhav and Ananya smiled and shook their heads.

"You find our conversation gripping because I am effectively communicating with you, serving you the platter you want at this point. This is the power of effective communication. Let me quote some statistics to turn your head around effective communication skills."

Sivaranjan continued, "Organizations with connected employees see 20-25% increase in productivity. Sixty-four percent of businesses prioritize communicating their strategy, values, and purpose to employees. Moreover, 97% of workers believe that communication has an impact on their daily tasks."

Vaibhav's eyes widened. "Wow, I had no idea communication had such a significant impact."

Ananya, who had been listening attentively, added, "I remember during our group projects in college, the teams that communicated well always outperformed the others. Clear roles and regular updates made a huge difference."

"Gallup research indicates that team members with higher levels of engagement produce significantly better results, improve customer service, attract new customers, are more likely to stay with their company, and are healthier and less likely to feel burnout. However, 69%

of managers are uncomfortable communicating with their employees, with 16% preferring email over face-to-face interactions," Sivaranjan said.

"That's quite surprising," Vaibhav admitted.

"Indeed. *According to one Gallup poll, only half of the employees understand what their managers expect of them. And 73% of employers prefer employees with strong communication skills.*"

"Now that we have all the information, let's understand it better in detail," said Sivaranjan.

What Are Effective Communication Skills?

"In today's interconnected world, the ability to communicate effectively with superiors, colleagues, and staff is indispensable," Sivaranjan explained. "Workers in the digital age must be able to effectively communicate and receive messages both in person and via phone, email, and social media. One of the most important life skills to learn is effective communication. Communication is defined as the transfer of information to produce greater understanding."

Vaibhav nodded. "I remember reading a quote by Harold Janis, an expert who said, 'The world of business is a world of action.' It emphasized the importance of communication in every aspect of business."

"Certainly," Sivaranjan agreed. "There is currently a high demand for people with strong communication skills. Every employer seeks employees with strong communication skills. Every interview is based on a test that demonstrates the candidate's effectiveness and clarity of communication skills. It has become critical for every organization to hire employees who excel in communication skills to maintain and build a good reputation in society."

"That makes a lot of sense," Vaibhav said. "I had a classmate who had been in a series of interviews since last semester and has been qualified in most of them. He has striking communication skills and confidence that certainly fit in any organization."

"That is the power of effective communication skills, Vaibhav," Sivaranjan said, smiling. "Let's delve into some essential communication skills that you can develop to stand out from the crowd."

Essential Communication Skills

"Want to land a top position at a prestigious company, just like that classmate?" Sivaranjan asked. "These are some of the most important communication skills that recruiters and hiring managers look for in resumes and cover letters. Highlight and demonstrate these skills during job interviews, and you'll make a good first impression. Continue to hone these skills after you've been hired, and you'll impress your boss, colleagues, and clients."

1. Active Listening

"Being a good listener is one of the most effective ways to communicate," Sivaranjan began. "No one enjoys conversing with someone who is only interested in adding their two cents and does not take the time to listen to the other person. Spend some time practicing active listening."

Ananya recalled, "In one of our seminars, a professor emphasized the importance of active listening. She had us pair up and practice by summarizing each other's points. It was eye-opening to see how much more engaged the conversation became."

Here are some more examples of active listening:

If I have understood you correctly: "If I have understood you correctly, you're saying that the new project deadline is next Friday, and we need to complete all the initial research by this Wednesday, right?"

Paraphrasing: "So, what I'm hearing is that you feel overwhelmed by the current workload and think it would be helpful to prioritize the tasks based on their deadlines."

Clarifying Questions: "Could you elaborate on what you meant by needing more resources? Are you referring to additional team members or better tools for the project?"

Reflecting Feelings: "It sounds like you're frustrated with the lack of communication from the team. Is that correct?"

Summarizing: "To summarize, you believe that improving our customer service training could lead to higher client satisfaction and better retention rates. Is that a fair summary of your point?"

Encouraging Elaboration: "Can you tell me more about your concerns regarding the new policy? I want to make sure I fully understand your perspective."

2. Nonverbal Communication

"According to UCLA Professor Albert Mehrabian, 93% of the information conveyed in communication is nonverbal," Sivaranjan said. "This includes body language, eye contact, hand gestures, and tone of voice."

"So, how we say something is often more important than what we say?" Vaibhav asked.

"Precisely," Sivaranjan affirmed. "Note: A relaxed, open stance (arms open, legs relaxed) and a friendly tone make you appear approachable and encourage others to speak freely with you."

Ananya shared, "I remember during presentations, I had to consciously work on making eye contact and using gestures and it helped me convey my message more effectively."

3. Body Language

"When communicating or listening, pay attention to your body language," Sivaranjan advised. "Open, relaxed shoulders and leaning forward indicate that you're engaged and open to new ideas, whereas folded arms and leaning back can make you appear distant and uninterested."

4. Verbal Communication

"It's not just about speaking, but also about understanding and responding to the work of others," Sivaranjan said. "Focus on both aspects to become a more well-rounded, effective communicator."

5. Empathy

"If you can put yourself in other people's shoes, you'll be able to understand how they feel and communicate with them more effectively," Sivaranjan explained. "This includes other employees, management, and your customers."

Ananya reflected, "During a group project, one of my teammates was struggling with personal issues. By empathizing and offering support, our team became more cohesive and productive."

6. The Attitude of Positivity

"A positive attitude makes life easier and nicer for you and those around you," Sivaranjan said. "If you're always upbeat, you're more likely to believe that things can be done and problems solved."

7. Giving and Receiving Feedback

"Being able to accept feedback gracefully helps a lot in moving forward after a problem," Sivaranjan noted. "Similarly, being able to provide excellent, positive feedback is a skill that can make anyone feel good."

Vaibhav recalled, "In our final project, we had peer evaluations. Positive feedback helped us improve our work significantly, and boosted our morale."

8. Be Concise

"There is no need to write an essay or give a speech to express an idea or make a point. Time is money in any business," Sivaranjan said. "Be brief, to the point, and only include necessary information. Follow up in writing so you have a copy of what you said for confirmation."

"Wow, these are incredible insights," Vaibhav said, his eyes shining. "I had a faculty member in college who I always looked up to for his astounding way of using words to glue us to the topic. We were able to register the topics in our minds for a long time."

"Communication skills enable you to effectively interact with others and make your presence felt by those present in a discussion or meeting," Sivaranjan said. "Being able to communicate effectively with your colleagues in a team will help you build trust, strengthen professional relationships, boost teamwork, develop a sense of belonging and become more productive. Without proper communication, even the best ideas can easily go unnoticed and, ultimately, wasted."

"Workplace success hangs in the balance with proper communication skills," Sivaranjan continued. "Being able to articulate effectively gives you a significant advantage. To do your job effectively, you must discuss problems, request information, interact with others, and have good interpersonal skills—all of which are components of good communication skills. They aid in being well-understood and in understanding the needs of those around you."

"This set me thinking and reflecting on my way of communication and how I interact with people around me," Vaibhav said thoughtfully. "I can see how crucial it is to improve these skills not just for professional success but for personal growth as well."

Ananya nodded in agreement. "Absolutely, Vaibhav. I remember when we had to organize a college event. Everyone knew their roles and responsibilities, and we were able to handle unexpected challenges. Now that I think of the success of that event, it could be because of our effective communication."

"That's a great example, Ananya," Sivaranjan said, smiling. "Effective communication is not just about talking but about understanding and being understood. It's about creating a bridge between people and ideas."

"I'll definitely work on these skills, Uncle," Vaibhav promised. "I can see how they are essential not just in the workplace but in all areas of life."

"That's the spirit, Vaibhav," Sivaranjan said warmly. "Remember, communication is a two-way street. It's not just about conveying your message but also about listening and understanding others. With practice and dedication, you'll find yourself becoming a more effective communicator, capable of making a positive impact wherever you go."

"Thank you for these insights, Uncle," Ananya added. "I'm excited to apply these principles in my interactions and see the difference they make."

"You're both on the right path," Sivaranjan said, nodding approvingly. ***"Keep learning, practicing, and refining your communication skills. It's a journey that will continually open new doors and opportunities for you."***

As they continued their discussion, Vaibhav and Ananya felt more equipped and motivated to embrace the power of effective communication. They understood that mastering these skills would not only help them excel in their careers but also enrich their personal lives, enabling them to build stronger relationships and achieve greater success in all their endeavors.

Express

Influence

Succeed

Chapter 3

Body Language

———— ✾ ————

"Like I said before, we as humans pay more than 90% of our attention to body language and tone of voice rather than actual words," said Sivaranjan, leaning forward with a gleam in his eye. "Words, body language, and tone of voice account for 7%, 55%, and 38% of effective communication, respectively, according to a study by body language expert Albert Mehrabian."

"Really," exclaimed Vaibhav and Ananya in sync, wide-eyed. "We would love to know more about it and reap the benefits in the long run."

"Wonderful. I appreciate the enthusiasm," said Sivaranjan, smiling. "Let's dig for the underlying gold and get a step closer to understanding and communicating with people even more effectively."

What is Body Language?

"Body language," Sivaranjan began, "is the language of the subconscious. It brings out our true feelings and makes our message more impactful. While good communication skills are essential for success in both professional and personal lives, it is the nonverbal cues or 'body language' that speak the loudest. Body language is the use of nonverbal communication through physical behavior, expressions, and mannerisms, which is often done instinctively rather than consciously."

"When we interact with others, whether we realize it or not, we are constantly sending and receiving nonverbal signals. All of our nonverbal behaviors—our gestures, posture, tone of voice, and amount of eye contact—send strong messages," he continued. "They can either put people at ease, build trust, and attract others to us, or they can offend, confuse, and undermine what we're trying to say."

Vaibhav nodded, absorbing every word. "It's fascinating how much we communicate without even realizing it," he mused.

"In some cases," Sivaranjan added, "what we say and what we communicate through our body language may be opposite. For example, if we say 'yes' while shaking our head no. When confronted with such conflicting signals, the other person will think whether to believe our verbal or nonverbal message. They will most likely choose the nonverbal message because body language is a natural, unconscious language that broadcasts our true feelings and intentions."

"Do you see how non-verbal communication impacts your communication?" asked Sivaranjan. "It might seem intimidating or overwhelming at the moment. However, once you unleash its power, you can connect better with others and crank up your relationships by expressing yourself better."

"Yes, uncle, now that I look back at my last interview, there were so many things I would have taken care of," Vaibhav admitted. "Nonetheless, I am here, learning it from the best."

"Thank you for the kind words, Vaibhav. Shall we continue?" Sivaranjan asked.

Vaibhav nodded eagerly.

Ananya added, "I remember once during a group project, I noticed that whenever someone disagreed, they would cross their arms or avoid eye contact. It was like an unspoken sign of tension. Understanding these cues could have helped us resolve conflicts more effectively."

Sivaranjan smiled at Ananya's observation. "That's a perfect example, Ananya. Let's delve into the most important non-verbal or body language cues."

Body Language is a Language of the Subconscious

"When you consciously pay attention to the body language of others, it means that you get reactions or unspoken emotions. However, you have to be

utterly vigilant to look out for the signs as they are a valuable form of feedback," said Sivaranjan. "Let us take a deep dive into the most important non-verbal or body language cues."

"Now with the rise of virtual meetings, especially on platforms like Zoom or Meet, how do we ensure our body language is effective even when we are not physically present?"

Ananya and Vaibhav looked at each other.

Sivaranjan continued. "Virtual communication has become an integral part of our professional lives, especially in the post-pandemic world. While it does pose some challenges, understanding and applying effective body language techniques can still make a significant difference."

Posture and Movement of the Body

"Consider how you perceive people based on how they sit, walk, stand, or hold their heads. The way you move and carry yourself conveys a wealth of information to the rest of the world. Your posture, bearing, stance, and subtle movements all contribute to nonverbal communication."

"Your posture is equally important in virtual meetings," Sivaranjan continued. "Sit up straight and lean slightly forward to show engagement and interest.

Avoid slouching or leaning back too much, as it can give the impression of disinterest or fatigue."

Ananya said, "I've noticed that sometimes people appear disengaged or distracted during Zoom calls, and it can affect the whole dynamic of the meeting."

Eye Contact

"Make direct eye contact because most people's dominant sense is vision, and eye contact is an especially important form of nonverbal communication," Sivaranjan advised. "The way you look at someone can convey a variety of emotions, such as interest, affection, hostility, or attraction. Maintaining eye contact is also important for keeping the conversation flowing and gauging the other person's interest and response."

"In a virtual setting, eye contact is crucial," Sivaranjan began. "To simulate direct eye contact, look into the camera rather than at the faces on your screen. This makes the other participants feel as though you are speaking directly to them."

Vaibhav nodded. "I never thought of that. I usually look at the screen, but it makes sense to look at the camera."

Facial Expressions

"The human face is extremely expressive and capable of conveying a wide range of emotions without saying a single word," he continued. "Facial expressions, unlike some other forms of nonverbal communication, are universal. Facial expressions of happiness, sadness, anger, surprise, fear, and disgust are universal."

"Even in virtual settings, facial expressions and gestures are important," Sivaranjan said. "Use your hands naturally when you speak to emphasize points, but be mindful not to overdo it, as it can be distracting. Your facial expressions should match your verbal messages to convey sincerity and enthusiasm."

Gestures

"Gesticulations are intertwined with our daily lives. When arguing or speaking animatedly, you may wave, point, beckon, or use your hands, often expressing yourself with gestures without thinking. However, the meaning of some gestures varies greatly across cultures. While the hand sign 'OK' conveys a positive message in English-speaking countries, it is considered offensive in countries such as Germany, Russia, and Brazil. It is critical to be careful with the use of gestures."

"Wow, that's interesting," said Vaibhav, reflecting on the cultural differences.

Voice

"It is not only what you say, but also how you say it. People 'read' your voice in addition to listening to

your words when you speak, "said Sivaranjan. "Your timing and pace, how loud you speak, your tone and inflection, and sounds that convey understanding, such as 'ahh' and 'uh-huh,' are all things they pay attention to. Consider how your tone of voice can convey sarcasm, anger, affection, or confidence."

Space

"Have you ever felt awkward during a conversation because the other person was standing too close to you and invading your personal space?" asked Sivaranjan. "We all require physical space, though the amount varies depending on culture, situation, and the closeness of the relationship. Physical space can be used to convey a variety of nonverbal messages like dominance or aggression and affection or intimacy."

Haptics or Touch

"We communicate a lot through touch. Consider the various messages conveyed by a weak handshake, a warm bear hug, a patronizing pat on the head, or a controlling grip on the arm."

"You see, Vaibhav," Sivaranjan continued, "people may come from a different cultural background than you, and positive gestures in one country may be considered negative in another. So, think about how you use body language and avoid making assumptions. If you're getting conflicting signals from someone, find out what they're thinking. After all, interpreting body language should be a supplement to talking and attentive listening, not a substitute for it."

Vaibhav gave a nod while sinking in all the information.

How to Enhance Your Body Language?

"Nonverbal communication is a fast-paced back-and-forth process that requires your complete attention to the present moment. If you're thinking about what you're going to say next, checking your phone, or doing something else, you're almost certain to miss nonverbal cues and not fully comprehend what's being communicated. In addition to being fully present, you can improve your nonverbal communication skills by learning to manage stress and increase your emotional awareness," said Sivaranjan.

Develop Emotional Awareness

"Being emotionally aware allows you to do the following," Sivaranjan began, leaning forward slightly to emphasize his points.

"Yes, Uncle?" Vaibhav replied, eager to learn more.

Sivaranjan continued, "You can read other people accurately, including the emotions they're feeling and the unspoken messages they're sending. This is crucial in both personal and professional settings."

"How do I improve this skill?" Vaibhav asked and turned to see if Ananya felt the same.

Ananya nodded.

"Creating trust in relationships is another benefit," Sivaranjan explained. "By sending nonverbal cues that correspond to your words, you show people that you're genuine and trustworthy. Also, respond in ways that demonstrate to others that you understand and care. This will enhance your connections significantly."

"I understand," Vaibhav nodded. "So, it's about being consistent and genuine with my actions and words."

"Indeed," Sivaranjan affirmed. "Many of us are disconnected from our emotions, particularly strong emotions like anger, sadness, and fear because we've been taught to suppress these emotions. But you can't get rid of them. They are still there and continue to influence your behavior."

"So, I need to acknowledge and understand these emotions?" Vaibhav asked.

"Yes, precisely," Sivaranjan said. "By increasing your emotional awareness and connecting with even the most unpleasant emotions, you'll gain more control over how you think and act."

Learn to Steer Your Stress

Sivaranjan continued, "Stress can leave you swamped, and it will compromise your ability to communicate effectively."

"How does stress affect communication?" Vaibhav inquired.

"You may end up being misread by people for sending confusing or off-putting nonverbal cues," Sivaranjan explained. "Take a break if you're feeling overwhelmed by stress. Take a moment to relax before re-joining the conversation."

"That makes sense," Vaibhav said thoughtfully. "So, I should find ways to calm myself during stressful moments?"

"Absolutely," Sivaranjan nodded. ***Using your senses—what you see, hear, smell, taste, and touch—or a soothing movement is the quickest and most reliable way to calm yourself and manage stress at the moment.*** You may need to experiment to find the sensory experience that works best for you because everyone responds differently."

"I'll definitely try that," Vaibhav said, jotting down notes.

"Vaibhav, in our early professional life, we often trip over stress and lose our grip on body language. Once you diligently practice and work on improving these factors, you will conquer any interview and will reign in any workplace," Sivaranjan added. "Body language is an important tool for communicating with those around you. It is important not only in everyday communication but also for the interpreter. ***Knowing how to read and use body language effectively explains why being at a loss for words isn't always a bad thing!***"

"I am glad, privileged, and humbled to get these treasures of insights from you, Uncle. I feel confident now, and these enlightening conversations have certainly amped me up for my corporate journey," said Vaibhav, his eyes shining with newfound confidence and determination.

Ananya, who had been listening attentively, chimed in, "Absolutely, Uncle Sivaranjan. Understanding these nuances in communication could have made a huge difference during our college years, especially in group projects and presentations. Sometimes, just a slight adjustment in how we presented ourselves could have changed the entire dynamic."

"Indeed, Ananya," Sivaranjan nodded, acknowledging her perspective. "Learning these skills early on prepares you for navigating various professional situations with confidence and clarity. It's about adapting and refining your communication style to fit different contexts and audiences."

Elegance
Boosts
Confidence

Chapter 4

Impact of Power Dressing

"Now, do you know the subtle art of standing out while fitting in at the workplace? How do you make yourself heard without words?" asked Sivaranjan, leaning back in his chair with a knowing smile.

"I'm not entirely sure, Uncle," Vaibhav admitted. "It sounds like a tricky balance to maintain."

"According to Abraham Putnick's research from California State University, formal clothing prompts people to think like leaders and make decisions more expansively and abstractly," Sivaranjan explained. "The findings were compared to those who made decisions based on immediate and pragmatic issues; these individuals wore casual clothing and placed less emphasis on appearance. As a result, we can conclude that formal attire is appropriate for people looking to advance in their careers. After all, the adage 'dress for the job you want, not the one you have' is timeless."

"That's interesting," said Ananya, nodding thoughtfully. "I always thought power dressing was just about looking sharp, but it seems there's a lot more to it."

"Since the 1970s, the concept of power dressing has been prevalent. When professionals are dressed powerfully, they are said to look their best," continued Sivaranjan. "However, the definition has evolved since the term was coined earlier. It was all about wearing fine, expensive clothing with sharp lines that made professionals appear more angular and assertive in the early ages. **Today, power dressing refers to a person's overall appearance. It is about how appropriately we dress for the occasion.**"

Ananya said, "Absolutely, Uncle. Understanding these nuances in communication could have made a huge difference during our college years, especially in the presentations. Sometimes, just a slight adjustment in how we presented ourselves could have changed the entire dynamic."

"Indeed, Ananya," Sivaranjan nodded, acknowledging her perspective. "Learning these skills early on prepares you for navigating various professional situations with confidence and clarity. It's about adapting and refining your communication style to fit different contexts and audiences."

"Uncle, I always thought power dressing or grooming depended on the way we dress for work," Vaibhav said with a sparkle in his eyes. "However, I am discovering some interesting facts about our overall presence in the workplace. It is a pragmatic journey for me and it can help so many others like me."

"Certainly, our conversations can ignite a spark in all those on the cusp of transformation," said Sivaranjan, smiling warmly. "Shall we dive deeper?"

What Is Power Dressing?

"Power dressing is an individual's distinct style that demonstrates their position and authority in business or at the workplace. When people advise you to dress for the position you want, they are correct because power dressing has a significant impact on your career," said Sivaranjan.

"Not only does your clothing matter, but so do your style, confidence, body language, and overall demeanor," he continued. "Although your clothing is not an indicator of your intelligence, it does serve as a confidence and morale booster in the workplace. When you have intelligence, intellectual ability, and leadership potential, your dressing style conveys this message in the best possible way. The charm and suaveness that power dressing exudes are unmistakable and extraordinary for people who want to make a name for themselves in climbing the corporate ladder."

"First impressions are peculiar; they never happen again," Vaibhav interjected thoughtfully. "We believe in talent and inner beauty; however, we cannot deny the importance of power dressing."

"Right," Sivaranjan agreed. ***"Your first presentation is your appearance, and if it is on point, your subsequent presentations in the boardroom are more likely to leave an impression.*** Your attire and demeanor in the workplace not only reflect your job description but also reveal the relationship between your mind, body, and soul. So, no matter how hard you try to avoid the eternal dilemma of 'What do I wear today?' you must plan your outfit before getting ready for a day at work."

What are the Power Ways to Enhance Your Presence?

"New-age businesses and start-ups take a more modern and realistic approach. "Today, plain tees could be worn at press conferences (only if you are a CEO of a multibillion dollar)," Sivaranjan chuckled. "Power dressing has blurred, however, there are unspoken rules about what to wear and what not to wear. Let's look at the advantages of power dressing."

"Power dressing is smart dressing," he emphasized. "The right attire can help you make a good first impression and even get you ahead at work. It serves as a window into your personality and influences how others perceive you."

Make Sure You Gel Well with the Attire

"Whether it's casual trousers with a T-shirt or an elegant suit, if it doesn't fit properly, it's not acceptable," Sivaranjan advised. "Don't just grab clothes from the rack and toss them into the cart. Choose them, try on different fits and colors, walk or try on comfortable postures, feel the fabric as power dressing becomes your image and identity. Your attire should accentuate your personality."

"Choose fabrics that accentuate your features," he continued. "The clothes you wear should look good when you stand or move around as well as when you sit. Tailored clothes are an all-time must-have because they fit perfectly to your body's curves and make you look your best."

Be Neat and Tidy

"With a tousled face, you can wear the best clothes and look dull. You must maintain your hair. A well-groomed hair gives you a literal advantage over others. Any outfit can be put together with a decent trim, and the best suits will look shabby if your grooming isn't up to par."

"I always notice that," Vaibhav agreed. "Sometimes, even a small grooming detail can make a big difference."

And Ananya, Sivaranjan said, "For women, it's not just about hair. Makeup should be subtle and appropriate for the setting. A clean, natural look often works best for the workplace. Well-maintained nails and minimal, tasteful accessories can also enhance your professional appearance. It's all about presenting a polished and composed image."

"Even paying attention to small details like having a lint-free outfit or ensuring your clothes are properly ironed can make a big difference," Sivaranjan added. "It shows that you take pride in your appearance and, by extension, your work."

It's Always About the Best Foot(wear)

"It is said, 'Good shoes take you to good places.' If you want to outdo your entrance in a new space, then always put your foot forward with the best footwear. Read the room and choose accordingly. Did you know that when you're on a date, a woman looks at your shoes first?" Sivaranjan added with a wink.

"Really? I never thought about that!" Ananya exclaimed, hesitantly looking at her sneakers.

"Always have a variety of shoes to wear on different occasions. It is not about the most expensive footwear you wear but the most appropriate as per the occasion," explained Sivaranjan.

"Even Steve Jobs, the minimalist, had a signature trainer, New Balance 991, to go with his black roll-neck. Every man's shoe closet should include a pair of well-polished leather shoes for formal occasions and a clean pair of sneakers for casual outings. Have formal shoes in both black and brown to match the accessories such as belts and watches."

"Please remember whatever the color of the shoe should be the color of the belt you are wearing. I have seen a lot of people not paying attention to this detail."

"How should it be for females, Uncle?" Ananya inquired, curiosity evident in her tone.

"For women, the principles are quite similar. The key is to choose footwear that complements your outfit and the occasion," Sivaranjan began. "For formal settings, a pair of classic pumps or heeled sandals in neutral colors like black, nude, or navy are ideal. They should be comfortable enough to wear throughout the day but stylish enough to make an impression."

"Ananya, you should also consider the height of the heels," he added. "In a professional setting, it's best to opt for mid-height heels that are elegant yet practical. For more casual occasions, a pair of well-maintained flats or stylish sneakers can work wonders. And remember, the condition of your shoes matters just as much as the style. They should always be clean and polished."

"That's good to know, Uncle," Ananya said, nodding thoughtfully. "I often struggle with finding the right balance between style and comfort."

"Another tip," Sivaranjan continued, "is to ensure your shoes match or complement your accessories, such as your handbag or belt. A cohesive look can significantly enhance your overall appearance. And just like with men, the color coordination between your shoes and other accessories is important. If you're wearing a black belt, black shoes are a safe bet. The same goes for other colors."

"Thanks, Uncle," Ananya replied with a smile. "I'll definitely keep these tips in mind."

Wear Your Confidence Up Your Sleeve

"A good watch personifies power dressing like no other true staple. Watches, cufflinks, brooches, rings, and other accessories help to elevate your brand. You don't have to wear all of these; instead, choose one or two and incorporate them into your style."

Bags to Brag

"You might be surprised to learn that power dressing includes bags. Assume you are dressed superbly from head to toe and are carrying a backpack. It's ruining your 'Oh, so Perfect' look. Similarly, if you simply replace the backpack with a sleek leather laptop bag, or a structured handbag, your boss may compliment the bag and notice you."

"In an official setting, a laptop bag is more professional, as is a duffle bag on business trips. Your backpacks are certainly short and comfortable (which is why kids use them), but they lack the elegance to add power to your outfit."

Sivaranjan continued. "The key is to find a bag that complements your outfit and serves its practical purpose without compromising on style. Opt for neutral colors like black, brown, or navy, which can match a variety of outfits."

"And pay attention to the material," Sivaranjan added. "A high-quality leather or faux leather bag can make a big difference in your overall appearance. It's also essential to ensure that your bag is well-maintained and free of wear and tear."

"See there, Vaibhav and Ananya, a recipe for your magical aura through the tactics of power dressing is ready," concluded Sivaranjan. "Your determination to make a difference in the corporate world will always be acknowledged, I am certain of that."

"Thank you for wishing us well, Uncle. Your faith in us is surely boosting our confidence," said Vaibhav cheerfully.

"***One thing about power dressing is that it's contagious.*** That is, if you decide to go the extra mile by paying more attention to detail in your professional attire, your co-workers are very likely to do the same eventually," said Sivaranjan.

"I can see how that works," Ananya agreed. "It sets a standard that others want to match."

"Vaibhav and Ananya, you have to tread this trail very cautiously. Your powerful outfits will create an extra impact and radiate strong power postures. 'Power dressing is about learning to present yourself most effectively; it's all about dressing in a way that conveys importance and success at the same time,' says Allen Flusser," quoted Sivaranjan.

"Got it, Uncle," Vaibhav replied. "I'll make sure to implement all these tips and see how they transform my professional life."

"Good luck, Vaibhav and Ananya," said Sivaranjan, patting their shoulders. "Remember, it's all about the confidence you carry within and how you choose to express it through your appearance."

Listen

Speak

Collaborate

Chapter 5

Effective Verbal Communication

"Vaibhav, Ananya, let me tell you a story of a professional who was the CEO of a renowned corporation," said Sivaranjan, leaning forward with an intent gaze. "His job responsibilities required him to make decisions in a matter of five minutes on projects going on for months. Due to the need for quick decision-making, he started using a rule: He approved the proposal if the person making it appeared confident. If not, he declined."

"That sounds like a reasonable approach, Uncle," Vaibhav interjected, looking curious. "But I sense there's a catch."

"It might appear to be reasonable," Sivaranjan nodded. "However, my beliefs suggest otherwise. The CEO believes he understands what a confident person sounds like. However, his decision, while correct for some, may be entirely incorrect for others."

"Why do you think that is?" Ananya asked, furrowing her brow.

"Communication conveys more than saying what you mean. Because language is a learned social behavior, how you say what you mean is critical and varies from person to person. Cultural experience has a significant impact on how we speak and listen. Although we may believe that our ways of saying what we mean are natural, we can get into trouble if we interpret and evaluate others as if they felt the same way we would if we spoke the same way they did."

"That makes a lot of sense," Vaibhav replied, nodding in agreement. "I've noticed that sometimes people misinterpret my intentions because of how I phrase things."

"According to a survey, *'Communication and interpersonal skills remain at the top of the list of what recruiters value the most.'* And I wonder, why do we ignore communication's importance until it becomes a problem?" Sivaranjan asked, raising an eyebrow.

"Perhaps, one reason could be that we are not conscious about the congruency in the way we speak, the way we project, and the choice of words," Ananya suggested thoughtfully.

"Exactly!" Sivaranjan exclaimed. "Today, we will deep dive into effective verbal communication."

What Is Verbal Communication?

"The act of sharing information between individuals through speech is known as verbal communication," Sivaranjan explained. "Verbal communication refers to any interaction that involves the use of spoken words. Personal conversations, staff meetings, phone conversations, formal and informal conversations, and presentations are all examples of verbal communication used within an organization."

"So, it's more than just talking," Ananya remarked. "It's about how you convey the message."

"Indeed," Sivaranjan affirmed. "Phone calls, face-to-face meetings, speeches, teleconferences, and video conferences are all examples of different ways of communication within and outside of the organization. Effective verbal communication skills enable managers to communicate more precisely with their subordinates. Employees with excellent communication skills are similarly highly valued and sought after in any organization."

"Vaibhav, Ananya, how you present yourself in any meeting and the mannerism with which you speak can impact your future in the organization," he continued. ***People who can articulate well and express themselves clearly always stand out.*** The organizations also want people who are fluent and well-versed to be their brand ambassadors because when you go and meet anyone, you are not representing yourself as an individual; you are speaking on behalf of your organization."

"That's a lot of responsibility," Vaibhav noted. "It's not just about me; it's about the company too."

"These are a couple of pointers to understanding the prominence of communication in any workplace," Sivaranjan said.

Importance of Verbal Communication

"Here are some key points to consider," Sivaranjan continued:

"The way employees communicate with one another reflects an organization's culture, which could be the first or last impression.

Good verbal communication skills foster excellent business relationships with other organizations, customers, suppliers, and so on.

Good verbal communication in the workplace is critical for companies with a diverse workforce. It aids in the reduction of barriers caused by cultural and linguistic differences. Many multinational corporations provide training to their employees to instil effective communication skills, which prove to be extremely beneficial in the long run.

Effective verbal communication between different stakeholders in the organization boosts job satisfaction.

Receiving up-to-date and accurate information from their superiors amplifies their productivity and confidence.

Individuals with excellent verbal communication skills are more likely to share ideas, thoughts, and concerns with one another."

"A good communicator becomes automatically visible in any organization, and it directly impacts your perception in the eyes of others," Sivaranjan emphasized. "Be mindful to consciously practice communication fluency and enhance your vocabulary."

"Understood, Uncle," Vaibhav responded. "But how do I improve my verbal communication skills?"

"That's a great question," Ananya added. "Especially since we both will have to present projects and ideas regularly. It can be challenging to get our points across effectively."

Constituents of Effective Verbal Communication

"It is unfathomable to find ourselves at work without verbal communication. There is so much to be done verbally, giving instructions, raising a query, making arrangements, and so on," said Sivaranjan. "The motive of communication at work is to build good relationships with stakeholders, co-workers, superiors, and customers, to be a part of an efficient team, and enhance your professional skills down the line."

"What are the key ingredients to achieve that?" Vaibhav inquired eagerly.

"These are a few ingredients to complete the recipe of effective verbal communication," Sivaranjan began.

Communication Fluency

"Just imagine, you are new in your company and you have a query, and you have no idea how to convey it to your team leader. This is where communication fluency plays an important role. It helps you exchange ideas, facts, feelings, and information, and channel your perspectives."

"Fluency is the concept and phenomenon of becoming skilled in a specific area. As a result, communication fluency is the act of becoming excellent in a conversation by learning all of the necessary elements and skills," Sivaranjan explained.

"Good communication skills are the most important factor in achieving success in the workplace," he added. "The reason for this is that effective communication is essential for increased sustainability."

Choice of Words

"People should choose their words to connect with others," according to Stacy Philpot, head of Deloitte Consulting's Leadership Practice. "The most influential leaders are those who consider how to energize their people," Philpot told Business News Daily. "They understand what makes their people feel confident and what drains their energy."

"Rather than discussing plans or tactical objectives, they can connect their employees' current circumstances to some kind of opportunity or outcome that they care about. The ever-changing business language necessitates executives who can approach their words with caution and care, and adapt their communication style as needed," Sivaranjan shared.

The Pace of Speech

"You probably are aware of RPM (Revolutions per minute), similarly there is a concept called WPM (Words per minute). According to research, **our WPM could be anything between 150-225 per minute (of course, there are exceptions).**"

"Pacing can be one of your most powerful tools," Sivaranjan continued. "The ultimate goal is to be able to talk at a conversational pace. Do not try to speak at a completely even pace, measuring out every word evenly:

this may come across as monotonous and boring. Your speech will be more engaging if you use a combination of slow, fast, and medium speeds."

Articulation

"The ability to express a thought clearly and effectively is referred to as articulation. The beginning of communication is articulation. Because your audience does not have subtitles or a pause button, it comes into focus when you speak," explained Sivaranjan.

"Deliver your message in as few words as possible. Writing is an excellent way to improve your articulation. Take notes on conversations or ideas. Read them slowly and aloud. Check to see if it feels right. This procedure will assist you in improving your verbal communication skills," he advised.

Pauses

"Now you might be wondering, 'How can silence make a conversation interesting?' It's not as simple as it sounds," Sivaranjan said with a smile. "It is difficult to practice silence at the right time and in the right place. Make a deliberate choice. Make a promise to yourself that you will pause. A well-chosen pause will assist you in better and more structured conversation construction."

"When negotiating, a well-timed pause will allow you to gain control of the situation more quickly. A pause relaxes your mind and body, making your conversation more meaningful and fruitful," he explained.

The Tone of Voice

"In communication, it can be defined as how a person speaks to others. Often, how you say something is just as important as what you say," Sivaranjan said. "You may adjust your tone of voice depending on whom you are speaking to and the context of the situation."

"The sound of your voice contains elements that add meaning to what you're saying. There are subtle nuances that change the meaning, whether spoken or unspoken. For example, two people may say the same thing, but the message is received differently if they use different vocal tones," he elaborated.

"It is just phenomenal the way different constituents come together to create a symphony of effective communication," Vaibhav exclaimed. "I am amazed to see the broad spectrum of communication and its hold over our individuality."

"Can you give us an example?" Ananya asked.

"Sure," Sivaranjan replied. "Imagine saying 'I'm fine' in a flat, monotonous voice versus a cheerful, upbeat tone. The same words can convey vastly different emotions and meanings depending on the tone."

Sivaranjan added, ***'Measure what you treasure,' as professionals say, refers to aligning rewards with corporate goals.*** Communication follows the same philosophy. You will recruit, train, and hire for communication skills if you value them. Verbal skills are a basic foundation; organizations must also consider how such skills are used to inform, persuade, coach, and inspire. Years of practice and examples are required. Leaders must set an example by communicating clearly and teaching others to do the same."

"Thank you, Uncle," Vaibhav said, feeling enlightened. "This has been incredibly insightful."

"Yes, thank you so much," Ananya added. "I feel more prepared to improve my communication skills."

"You're welcome," Sivaranjan replied with a warm smile. "Remember, communication is an art that can always be refined. Keep practicing, stay mindful, and you'll see remarkable improvements."

Compose
Captivate
Convey

Chapter 6

Written Communication - Art or Science?

"Vaibhav, Ananya, do you know that our brain scans show in peculiar detail what persuades us as readers?" Sivaranjan began. *"Scientists have observed a group of midbrain neurons known as the 'reward circuit' light up in response to anything from a simple metaphor to an unexpected story twist.* What's the takeaway? You can write in a way that entices readers on a primal level, releasing pleasure chemicals in their brains, whether you are writing an email to a colleague or an important report for the board."

"Wow, I had no idea writing could have such a profound effect on the brain," said Vaibhav, intrigued.

"Yes," Sivaranjan replied with a knowing smile. "Strong writing skills are essential for anyone working in business. You'll need them to communicate effectively with colleagues, employees, and bosses, as well as to snap up ideas, products, or services you're offering.

So, we are going to board the plane of effective written communication in the workplace."

"That sounds fascinating, uncle. I'm ready to learn more," V0aibhav responded enthusiastically.

"Me too, Uncle," Ananya chimed in. "I've always struggled with getting my point across clearly in emails and reports."

What is Effective Written Communication?

"Many people, particularly in the business world, believe that good writing is an art and that those who do it well have an innate talent they've developed through experience, intuition, and a habit of reading widely and frequently," Sivaranjan began.

"But we're learning more about the science of good writing every day," he continued. "Neurobiology and psychology advances show, with data and images, how the brain responds to words, phrases, and stories. And, contrary to popular belief, the criteria for making better writing choices are more objective than you might think. Good writing causes dopamine to flow in the reward circuit of the reader's brain. Great writing releases opioids, which activate reward hotspots."

"So, it's not just about what you write but how you write it?" Ananya asked.

"Absolutely," said Sivaranjan. "Just like good food, a relaxing bath, or a warm hug, a symphony of words melt in your brain and keeps you glued to the write-up. Whether it is a complex argument in a report, a succinct declarative statement in an email, or a heart-warming concern in a letter, your writing has the flair to mitigate the neural net of your readers' brains."

What are the Characteristics of Effective Written Communication?

"Given the importance of reading and writing comprehension in our virtual and real lives, it's time to remind ourselves what constitutes good communication," Sivaranjan continued. ***Reading carefully is the new listening, and writing is the new empathy, as described in the book Digital Body Language.***

"The magic happens when your write-up is a perfect blend of one or more of these characteristics or so to say the seven C's being the hallmarks of compelling writing," he explained.

"Seven C's?" Vaibhav and Ananya repeated in unison, eager to learn more.

"Yes," Sivaranjan nodded. "Let's go through them."

Concise

"Scientists refer to this as the brain's 'processing fluency.' Short sentences, familiar words, and clean syntax ensure that the reader does not have to work too hard to grasp your meaning," Sivaranjan said.

"For instance," he continued, "if you write 'Profits are loved by investors,' rather than 'Investors love profits,' you're flipping the verb and direct object positions. This can reduce comprehension accuracy by 10% and make reading take a tenth of a second longer."

"That's a subtle but significant difference," Ananya noted.

"It is," Sivaranjan agreed. "Tsuyoshi Okuhara of the University of Tokyo collaborated with colleagues to ask 400 people between the ages of 40 and 69 to read about how to exercise for better health. Half of the group received lengthy, somewhat technical material. The other half received an easier-to-read version of the same content. The group that read the simplified version— which had shorter words and sentences, among other things—scored higher on self-efficacy: they were more confident in their ability to succeed."

"That's impressive," Vaibhav remarked. "It shows the power of concise writing."

"I remember struggling with long and complicated texts during our courses, Vaibhav," Ananya added. "This makes so much sense now."

Clarity

"Your readers will benefit from more vivid, clear, and noticeable language," Sivaranjan explained. "Amazon CEO Jeff Bezos did not say in a recent letter to shareholders, 'We're facing strong competition.' Instead, he wrote, 'Third-party sellers are kicking our first-party butts. Badly.' Even though some of us might find the choice of words offensive, this is one of the ways of conveying what you are feeling."

"Clarity stimulates a wide range of brain circuits," he continued. "Consider the terms pelican and bird, or 'wipe' versus 'clean.' According to one study, the more specific words used in pairs activated more neurons in the visual and motor-strip areas of the brain than the general ones, causing the brain to process indications more vigorously."

"I see," Vaibhav said thoughtfully. "Being specific and clear can really be a game-changer."

"I once had to write a project proposal, and I struggled with making it clear and specific," Ananya reflected. "This would have been so helpful."

Correct

"Vaibhav and Ananya, your words should be as solid as concrete, and facts are the essence of a concrete write-up," Sivaranjan advised. "Fact-checking and re-checking before presenting them is a critical component of effective leadership. Be wary of framing opinions as facts. Your team and colleagues may take what you say as law, so make it as factual as possible."

"Absolutely," Vaibhav agreed. "Accuracy is crucial."

"And it can save us from a lot of trouble," Ananya added.

Concrete

"Great leaders can rally their troops simply by opening their mouths," Sivaranjan said with a grin. "The key to engaging people is the language used. Instead of general explanations, use descriptive words and phrases. Words should evoke images in the minds of the recipients."

"When you integrate stories into your communications, you can reap significant benefits," he continued. "Consider Melissa Lynne Murphy's research at the University of Texas on business crowdfunding campaigns. She discovered that participants in the study had more favorable impressions of pitches with richer

narratives, giving them higher marks for entrepreneur credibility and business legitimacy."

"Participants in the study also expressed a greater willingness to invest in the projects and share information about them," he added. "The implication is that without stories, there will be no significant funding success."

"Stories are powerful tools," Vaibhav acknowledged.

"And they make information more memorable," Ananya said. "I always remember stories from lectures better than plain facts."

Courteous

"You have to make sure that you write the way you would like to read," Sivaranjan said. "Being polite and showing your audience that you respect them can help you improve the effectiveness of your communications. Your messages should be formal, open, welcoming, considerate, respectful, and truthful. To help ensure that you are courteous, always use empathy and consider your messages from the perspective of the audience."

"The late Max De Pree, founder, and CEO of Herman Miller had a talent for speaking to employees in this manner," he continued. "The first responsibility of a leader is to define reality," he wrote in Leadership Is an Art. "The final step is to express gratitude. The leader must become a servant and a debtor between the two."

"That is sound advice not only for business executives but also for parents, teachers0, coaches, and anyone in a position of authority," Sivaranjan added.

"Being courteous is fundamental, noted!" Vaibhav said.

"And it can make a big difference in how your message is received," Ananya added. "People are more likely to respond positively."

Coherent

"A coherent conversation makes sense and flows logically," Sivaranjan explained. "Consider the order of your points and how you can understandably present them. When delivering multiple forms of communication, it is also critical to maintain consistency in style and content."

"How can you write so that your readers have an aha moment?" he asked. "One approach is to make new distinctions. Ginni Rometty, the former CEO of IBM, provided one with this future description: *'It will not be a world of man versus machine; it will be a world of man plus machine.'*"

"That's a powerful distinction," Vaibhav noted.

"And it brings a different perspective to light," Ananya added.

Complete

"Make sure you jot down everything needed in your write-up beforehand, like an overview or write-up structure," Sivaranjan advised. "As Marwin Swift said, 'Clear writing means clear thinking.' You might have all the great ideas and thoughts in the world, but if your write-up doesn't make sense or leaves your readers astray, there is a fair chance that the readers may lose interest. Effective written communication is not a gift you are born with; it is a skill that you cultivate to keep moving forward."

"Complete communication ensures that the readers have all of the information they require and can easily reach the desired conclusion," he continued. "Among the many ways to be complete are:

Including a 'call to action,' or what you want your audience to do after receiving the message.

Incorporating hyperlinks into the written content to ensure that all information is available."

"The seven C's can be your secret weapon when it comes to writing well," Sivaranjan concluded. "Since they elicit the same neural responses as other pleasurable stimuli, they are effective tools for engaging readers. You probably recognize their worth intuitively because millions of years of evolution have conditioned our brains to recognize what feels right. So feed those instincts. They'll lead you to the writer's version of the Golden Rule: Reward readers in the same way that you would reward yourself."

"I hope you both understand what glues written communication together," Sivaranjan asked.

"Yes, we do, Uncle," they replied in unison.

"It is something we indulge in every day, yet it is a mystery we discover by working at it consistently," Vaibhav added. "That is why it is the real work of leadership, and you have collected these gems by investing time in learning the skills meticulously."

Ananya said, considering the impact of effective communication on her future endeavors, "Learning about the science behind good writing is fascinating because it shows that there's a method to creating engaging content. It's not just about words on paper; it's about crafting an experience for the reader, whether you're presenting ideas, sharing information, or even telling a story."

Ananya glanced at Vaibhav and smiled, realizing they both shared a newfound appreciation for the art and science of communication. "Thank you for sharing these insights, Uncle. I'm looking forward to applying these principles in future."

Sivaranjan nodded warmly. "You're welcome, Ananya. **Remember, effective communication is a skill that can be honed over time.** By integrating these principles into your writing, you'll not only convey your ideas more clearly but also engage your audience more effectively."

Clear
Concise
Courteous

Chapter 7

Email Etiquette

"Do you know Ray Tomlinson?" Sivaranjan asked, looking up from his notes.

Vaibhav looked at Ananya, they both had no idea. "Who is he, uncle?"

"He's a well-known computer programmer credited with inventing email on the ARPANET system, the Internet's predecessor," Sivaranjan explained. "He changed the way businesses and people communicated all over the world. The new communication tool took the world by storm."

"Wow! I can't imagine a world without emails," Vaibhav remarked.

"Indeed," Sivaranjan nodded. "Today, nearly 4 billion email accounts exist, with email being used by half of the world's population. Tomlinson once said, 'In general, I see email being used exactly as I envisioned. *It's not just a work tool or a personal thing, in particular, everyone uses it in different ways.*

However, they all use it in ways that work for them.' It's true, every individual uses emails in their peculiar ways."

"That's fascinating. But why is email etiquette so important, uncle?" Ananya inquired.

Why Is Email Etiquette Important?

"According to a study by Adobe Systems, the average worker spends 6.3 hours per day sifting through and responding to emails. That's more than 30 hours per week or 63 full days per year," Sivaranjan explained. "You'd think that all of our practices would have made us experts in the art of email communication, but many professionals continue to get it wrong."

Vaibhav frowned. "Like how?"

"Accidental 'reply all' on a private email occurs far more frequently than HR departments would like to deal with. And how often do you receive emails that are irrelevant, inappropriate, or aggressive?" Sivaranjan asked.

Ananya nodded, recalling instances of unclear emails or accidental 'reply all' mishaps among classmates.

"Too often," Vaibhav admitted.

"Unfortunately, unless you use an email service provider and you catch your error within 10 seconds of sending it, you can't 'unsend' a poorly written email.

Otherwise, there is no way to prevent damage once the email is already in the recipient's inbox," Sivaranjan said.

"That sounds like a nightmare," Vaibhav said, wide-eyed.

"It can be," Sivaranjan agreed. "As computer networks are increasingly being used to organize and transmit information, the demand for competent writing skills is increasing. Dr. Craig Hogan, a former University Professor who now runs an online Business Writing School, receives hundreds of inquiries each month from managers and executives seeking assistance in improving their own and their employees' writing skills."

"So, what can be done to improve email etiquette?" Ananya asked eagerly.

"Email etiquette is the code of conduct that governs one's behavior when writing and/or responding to emails. These principles are designed to show professionalism and mutual respect among those exchanging emails," Sivaranjan began. "Let's go over some rules for email etiquette."

"Sure," Vaibhav and Ananya said, leaning forward, all set to jot down the notes.

What are the Rules for Email Etiquette?

"In the business world, you probably will write a lot, Vaibhav: memos to senior executives, proposals to clients, and a consistent flow of emails to colleagues. But how can you make your writing as clear and effective as possible? How do you get a top hand in the game of written communication," said Sivaranjan.

Rules for Email Etiquette:
Think before you write

"Consider what you want to say before putting pen to paper or fingers to keyboard. 'The mistake that many people make is that they begin writing too soon,' Bryan Garner, author of *The HBR Guide to Better Business Writing*, says. 'They work out their thoughts as they write, which results in less structured, meandering, and repetitive writing.'"

"So, I should gather my thoughts first?" Vaibhav asked.

"Yes. Consider what your audience should know or think after reading this email, proposal, or report. If the answer isn't obvious right away, take a step back and spend more time gathering your thoughts," Sivaranjan advised.

Make your subject line clear and professional

Make it clear to your recipient what the email will cover. Many people will decide whether or not to open an email based on its subject line. A concise subject line makes it easier for someone who receives hundreds of emails per day to sort through their inbox and decide which communications to prioritize.

"Got it. Clear and concise," Ananya nodded.

Write your email and then enter the recipient's email address

"It's a good idea to write the contents of your email first in case you accidentally send it too soon."

"I've done that before," Vaibhav admitted sheepishly.

Be certain to CC all relevant recipients

"It's improper to exclude a colleague or client from a relevant email chain. Consider who should be informed about a specific conversation and respect that."

"That makes sense," Vaibhav said thoughtfully.

In academic settings, including all group members ensures transparency," Ananya suggested.

Check that you have the correct recipient

"Imagine you sent the mail and it got an incorrect recipient or sent a confidential document to the wrong client or company. It could put your credibility in question."

Sending sensitive information to the wrong person can be disastrous," Vaibhav acknowledged.

Respond to your emails

"Most people feel overwhelmed by the large number of emails they have to sort through at some point. However, responding to an email is proper etiquette, especially if the sender expects a response."

"Even if it's just to acknowledge receipt?" Vaibhav asked.

"Even for that. Acknowledging that you received the email but will contact the sender later is a more professional option than ignoring or avoiding certain emails," Sivaranjan confirmed.

Change your default settings from 'reply all' to 'reply'

"This is a risk-averse technique to avoid any mistake made in a rush."

"I'll do that right away," Vaibhav said, making a note.

Change the 'undo send' option to 30 seconds

"Murphy's law states that when it comes to email in the workplace, you will always catch your mistakes 10 seconds after the email has been sent."

"Why not give yourself more time to catch errors?" Vaibhav nodded.

"Giving yourself a buffer can prevent mistakes," Ananya noted.

Use the proper level of formality

"When writing an email, begin with the appropriate salutation, such as 'Dear Mr./Ms. [Surname],' 'Sir,' or 'Ma'am.'"

"What about with friends?" Vaibhav asked.

"Emails sent to friends are likely to differ significantly from those sent to co-workers. Always close your email with a suitable sign-off, such as 'Kind regards,' 'Thank you,' or 'Sincerely,'" Sivaranjan explained.

Proofread all your emails before sending

"Check for any grammatical, punctuation, or professional errors. Use simple sentence structures and proper capitalization and punctuation."

"Correcting errors enhances professionalism," Ananya emphasized.

"I'll make sure to do that," Vaibhav promised.

Add a signature block

"It is appropriate to include your full name, title, company, and phone number."

"That adds credibility," Vaibhav noted.

Ananya nodded.

Keep your emails short and to the point

"People appreciate short, crisp, and apt emails."

"Less is more," Vaibhav repeated.

Sivaranjan smiled. "Nice choice of words. You can always follow up later or suggest they call you if they have any questions or concerns."

"Uncle, we too use email as students," Vaibhav said. "Once, I was amidst a never-ending email back and forth with two of my classmates. It seemed like we were having a circular written dialogue, covering the same ground over and over without understanding the context."

"What would you have done in that situation?" Ananya asked.

"If it was me, I would have got both of them on the phone, asked a few questions in a variety of ways, and drilled to the bottom of the problem," Sivaranjan suggested.

"That's a good idea. If I receive a vague or confusing text or email, I should not be afraid to request a phone call or, if possible, a video or in-person meeting," Vaibhav added.

"If it's a sensitive conversation, requesting a quick call demonstrates that you're being considerate," Sivaranjan agreed. ***"Waiting for a few beats before*** *responding to questions shows the other person that you are listening and taking your work seriously, rather than making you appear indecisive."*

Ananya and Vaibhav exchanged knowing looks, recognizing the relevance of these guidelines in both academic and future professional contexts.

"I appreciate these insights, uncle," Ananya said gratefully. "Understanding email etiquette will undoubtedly benefit us in college and beyond."

Sivaranjan nodded. "Mastering these skills early will serve you well. Effective communication is foundational in every aspect of life."

Inspire
Unite
Thrive

Chapter 8

Value of Values in Our Lives

"Before we take the plunge, let's start with a tale," Sivaranjan began.

"Sure, uncle. I'm all ears," Vaibhav replied.

Ananya, seated next to Vaibhav, leaned in. "I love your stories, Uncle. They always have such deep meanings."

"There was an elderly carpenter who was about to retire. He told his employer about his retirement plan to say goodbye to the business and have free rein with his family. He said he would surely miss his pay check; however, he needed retirement. His employer was deplorable to bid adieu to his favorite worker. So, he asked him to build one last house as a personal favor," Sivaranjan narrated.

"Did the carpenter agree?" Vaibhav asked.

"Yes, but the carpenter's mind, body, and soul were already in retirement mode. One last project seemed like wheels within wheels to him. He could not wrap his head around the work, resorted to shoddy workmanship, and used low-grade material. His objective was to finish the work and go back to his original plan for retirement," Sivaranjan continued.

"Oh no! That doesn't sound good," Ananya exclaimed, frowning.

"Indeed. When he finished the project and handed the keys to the house to his employer with a sigh of relief, his boss inspected the house and, with a smile on his face, handed the keys back to him, saying, 'This is your parting gift. Congratulations, it is your house,'" Sivaranjan explained.

"The carpenter must have been astounded!" Vaibhav remarked, wide-eyed.

"He was awestruck for a moment, thinking how differently he could have built the house if only he knew he was going to own it," Sivaranjan said.

"What do you learn from this story, Vaibhav? Ananya?" Sivaranjan asked.

"I think if he thought of it as the last project of his career, he could have given his heart and soul to it and remembered it as his biggest achievement for the rest of his days," Vaibhav reflected.

Ananya nodded, adding, "And it shows how important it is to always put in our best effort, no matter what."

"Indeed! If he loved, valued, and well-thought of his work, he would have given his 100%, last project or not. **Love is work made visible,**" Sivaranjan stated.

"That's a powerful lesson," Vaibhav acknowledged.

"It all boils down to the values we put on the top shelves of our lives. Our values reflect what means the most to us and what guides us throughout our entire lives. Our values are our personal guiding principles or life goals that guide our behavior in all aspects of our lives, including our lives at home, at work, and in society. **The significance of values stems from their purpose, which is to guide our behaviors, feelings, attitudes, and beliefs,**" Sivaranjan elaborated.

"Uncle, what are the dots that connect behaviors, feelings, attitudes, and beliefs?" Vaibhav queried.

"Let's deep dive into the matter at hand," Sivaranjan said.

"I'm ready," Vaibhav and Ananya nodded.

What is the Origin of Values?

"What we do and how we act constitute our behavior. This could include physical activities such as running and jumping, verbal behavior such as saying things we later regret, or complex behaviors such as cheating on a test or planning a party. Behaviors differ from thoughts and emotions in that they concern what we do in the world.

Thoughts and emotions, on the other hand, exist within us and do not require us to act on them," Sivaranjan explained.

"So, behaviors are actions, while thoughts and emotions are internal?" Vaibhav asked.

"Exactly. Behavior is an action performed by an individual that is tagged by others based on their perspective. The irony is that people get tags based on others' ideologies. If the action is good in their eyes, the behavior is good, and if the action is bad, the behavior is bad. We have to be cognitive enough to understand where these behaviors come from. As an example, when we watch a cricket match, our behavior swings like a pendulum depending on how the team we support is playing. The game is most likely taking place hundreds of miles away; however, our behavior dangles on the game of the team we are supporting," Sivaranjan elaborated.

"So our behaviors are influenced by external factors like sports events?" Vaibhav asked.

"Yes. Feelings influence our behavior. If our feelings are strong, they show in our actions; if our feelings are weak, they show in insignificant actions or behavior. We act differently toward those we like than those we dislike. Understanding the feelings that underpin and produce human behavior is the key to understanding it," Sivaranjan continued.

"That makes sense. What about attitudes?" Ananya inquired.

"Attitudes are defined by psychologists as a learned tendency to evaluate things in a particular way. This includes assessments of people, issues, objects, or events. Such assessments are frequently positive or negative, but they can also be ambiguous at times. 'Attitudes are caught, not taught,' as the saying goes. Three factors shape one's attitude: society, education, and the environment in which one grows up," Sivaranjan explained.

"Can you give an example?" Vaibhav asked.

"Consider this: a believer entering a Hindu temple, a Sikh temple/Gurudwara, or a Mosque will remove their footwear, wash their feet and hands, and then enter to pray, whereas it is perfectly acceptable to walk into a church with your shoes on. We are entering into a praying area in all four places; however, there is a slight difference in attitude to the same activity," Sivaranjan illustrated.

"That's interesting. And what about beliefs?" Ananya questioned.

"Beliefs are a fascinating topic that has been studied since time immemorial. Belief is the state of mind in which a person believes something to be true, with or without empirical evidence to prove that something is true with factual certainty. Another way to define belief is as a mental representation of a positive attitude toward the likelihood of something being true. We believe something to be true because we have faith in it. For example, I believe that lowering wages improves cost efficiency. Beliefs are formed through previous experience and other forms of learning," Sivaranjan elaborated.

"So, beliefs are deeply personal and can shape our actions and decisions?" Ananya noted, reflecting on her experiences.

"Yes, they can. ***In the professional world, it is vital to understand and be aware of the beliefs of the people and respect them as there is nothing right or wrong about them.*** While we are not always aware of our values, understanding them can help us make better decisions that will benefit us and others in the long run. This could imply taking a job with more opportunities for variety, change, and spontaneity, as opposed to one with more opportunities for security and tenure," Sivaranjan explained.

"That's insightful. How do these elements come together to form our values?" Vaibhav asked.

"At their core, the order of values depends on priorities. For example, someone may prioritize freedom over comfort and equality over comfort. This importance hierarchy corresponds to the belief that, if necessary, one thing (equality) should be sacrificed for another (comfort), and then another (comfort) for another (freedom)," Sivaranjan explained.

"So, behavior, feelings, attitudes, and beliefs congregate to bring out our values?" Ananya summarized and Vaibhav looked at her.

"Yes. This is the essence of how our values influence us through our words and actions. They assist us in growing and developing to create the future we desire for ourselves and others. Clarity about our values can help us build a solid life foundation, giving us a foundation for decision-making and preparing us for happiness in both life and work," Sivaranjan said.

"This has certainly given me a perspective to deep dive into my values, and I will work on exploring and making them the anchor of my life," Vaibhav reflected.

Ananya nodded, adding, "Me too, Uncle. I think understanding my values better will help me navigate life more effectively and prepare me for the future."

"Fair enough. Now shall we proceed to understand the upper hand of values in the workplace?" Sivaranjan asked.

"Sure, uncle. Let's unveil the treasure of values," Vaibhav agreed.

"Yes, I'm eager to learn more," Ananya chimed in.

Prominence of Values in the Workplace

"Recognizing, understanding, and adhering to your values is one of the most important efforts any human being can make, and it is equally important in the workplace. Values are significant because they shape our beliefs, attitudes, feelings, and behavior. The consequences of consistently compromising your values in your decision-making are undeniable," Sivaranjan explained.

Values help you get what you want

Sivaranjan began, "The purpose of your values spirals around every aspect of your life. They can be pivotal in the workplace, informing job searches and career decisions. To determine your work values, arrange them on the scale of most important to least important. These could include accomplishment, recognition, help, independence, working conditions, and justice. You will be able to identify companies or industries with methods and goals most conducive to your values if you have a clear sense of the values that deem fit in your work efforts."

"So, values guide us in choosing the right job and career path?" Vaibhav asked.

"Absolutely," said Sivaranjan.

Values keep you focused, motivated, and engaged

"When you work for a company whose product, process, or mission is not congruent at the individual level, productivity suffers. Living according to your values keeps you motivated and happy in all aspects of your life, including your job. Working towards a goal you don't strongly believe in can leave you lagging in your efforts, losing motivation much faster than if you were to truly want to strive for the goal in question," Sivaranjan explained.

"That makes a lot of sense," Vaibhav said, nodding. "I've felt that way during some of my projects at college. The ones I cared about the most were the ones I did the best on."

"I can relate to that too," Ananya added. "When I was part of the environmental club, I was so passionate about our projects that I put in extra hours without feeling tired."

"Exactly," said Sivaranjan.

Values help you make decisions

"Values are like a compass in one's life and simple decision-making tools, if one may want to use them as. If I have to make a decision and that decision is in line with what I believe and my values are, I become committed to the decision. When the outcome is

not in line with what I believe and my values are, I don't want to do it. Hence, values act as a simple decision-making tool," Sivaranjan reiterated.

"That definitely sounds like a useful approach," Vaibhav agreed. "It would make decision-making a lot clearer."

"It would save a lot of time agonizing over choices," Ananya commented.

Values are an infallible way of gaining self-respect

"If you value punctuality, let your coworkers know. Speak up if you believe your superiors are underappreciating or ignoring you. People will respect you if you respect yourself by sticking to what you believe is morally sound and in line with your values. Expressing your values enhances not only your relationships and happiness with others but also gives your self-esteem the front seat," Sivaranjan advised.

"So, expressing my values can actually enhance my relationships and happiness at work?" asked Vaibhav.

"Yes, you have to understand the fact that others' values vary from your own is core to better understand others. Values can help us predict each other's choices, which can help us avoid misunderstandings, frustration, and distrust. People prioritize different sets of values that guide their behavior while their choices may differ from yours, but there is nothing wrong with them," Sivaranjan explained.

Character Strengths and Values

"To add another layer, let's talk about character strengths and how they align with values. Character strengths are positive traits reflected in thoughts, feelings, and behaviors. They are the psychological ingredients for displaying virtues or human goodness. These strengths include wisdom, courage, humanity, justice, temperance, and transcendence," Sivaranjan continued.

"How do these strengths connect to our values?" Ananya asked.

"Character strengths are the means through which we express our values. For example, if you value honesty, your strength might be integrity, which ensures that you act in accordance with your values. If you value kindness, your strength could be compassion, helping you to consistently treat others with care and empathy. Understanding your character strengths can help you see how you can live out your values more fully in daily life," Sivaranjan explained.

"So, recognizing our strengths can help us align more closely with our values?" Vaibhav inquired.

"Exactly. Knowing your character strengths allows you to leverage them in situations that matter to you.

This not only helps you stay true to your values but also boosts your confidence and satisfaction," Sivaranjan added.

"Uncle, how can we find out our strengths?" Vaibhav asked.

"That's a great question, Vaibhav," Sivaranjan responded. "There's a useful tool that can help you identify your character strengths. You can take the VIA Survey of Character Strengths. It's a scientifically validated survey that will help you understand your unique strengths."

"Where can we take this survey?" Ananya inquired.

"You can access it online. Here is the link: VIA Character Strengths Survey. This will give you insights into your core strengths and how you can use them to align with your values," Sivaranjan explained.

"Thanks, Uncle! We'll definitely check it out," Vaibhav said eagerly.

"Yes, this will be very helpful," Ananya added.

As we conclude, this is how our values influence us through our words and actions. They assist us in growing and developing to create the future we desire for ourselves and others. Clarity about our values can help us build a solid life foundation, giving us a foundation for decision-making and preparing us for happiness in both life and work," said Sivaranjan.

"This has certainly given me a perspective to deep dive into my values, and I will work on exploring and making them the anchor of my life," said Vaibhav with a spark in his eyes.

"Me too, Uncle. I think understanding my values better will help me navigate my career choices more effectively and prepare me for the future," Ananya added.

"That's a wise approach. Understanding and living by your values will truly set you on the path to both personal and professional fulfilment, smiled Sivaranjan.

As they got up to leave, Sivaranjan added, "Vaibhav, Ananya, it's been a pleasure watching you grow and learn. Your journeys are just beginning, and I believe you both will achieve great things. Always remember to stay true to yourselves and your values."

"Thank you, Uncle. We will," Vaibhav and Ananya said in unison, feeling inspired by Sivaranjan's words.

Note: We have no affiliation to the VIA Survey of Character Strengths, however, we find it insightful. Feel free to take the survey if you wish.

Believe
Think
Act

Chapter 9

Importance of Building Habit

———◆◆———

"I will take it that you both know Elon Musk. He is best known for developing electric cars (Tesla) and building spaceships (SpaceX). He wishes to hack the human mind for us to live inside the Matrix (Neuralink). Although he is a 49-year-old, he is already more successful than a million average people combined," asked Sivaranjan

"Yes, Uncle. Elon Musk is a name synonymous with innovation and relentless pursuit of goals. But how does he manage to stay so focused and driven?" Vaibhav asked.

"And why is it that despite having the same 24 hours in a day, he accomplishes so much more than most people?" Ananya added.

"There is no easy answer to prove the possibility of his success. It's mostly due to his superhuman willpower. However, his vigour for success laid the most groundwork for him. To keep the ball in his court with being the world's richest man, he follows a jam-packed schedule. It is said that he clocks to work for 80-100 hours per week, which is about 12-13 hours per day," Sivaranjan explained.

"That's incredible! But what do you think keeps him going and keeps his focus through and through?" Vaibhav inquired.

"Habits! It is his habits that help him manage his time and priorities and give him the spur to soar high with success. A few habits that he follows every day as a ritual are:

- He is an early bird and makes sure to hit the bed early to have adequate sleep.

- His mantra is to eat to live and not the other way around.

- He barely uses his phone during work hours to give his undivided attention to his work.

- He is a voracious reader, and despite his busy schedule, he makes time for reading," Sivaranjan elaborated.

"Wow, that's quite a regimen. I've heard that reading can have numerous benefits," Ananya remarked.

"Indeed. Studies show that reading improves comprehension and analytical skills. It not only stimulates the imagination but also the memory centers of the mind. It's no surprise that Musk is regarded as one of the greatest innovators of all time," Sivaranjan agreed.

"It makes sense now. Our habits really do take the biggest room in our lives," Vaibhav noted.

"Exactly. If we work on our habits consciously, they can help us emerge as the individuals we often dream about. So, what are habits?" Sivaranjan asked.

What are Habits?

"Habits are behaviors and rituals that we perform as a matter of course, right?" Vaibhav responded.

"Correct. They allow us to do things like our daily chores or taking the same routes every day without thinking about it. Our unconscious habits free up resources in our brains for more complex tasks like problem-solving or deciding what to make for dinner," Sivaranjan explained.

"That's fascinating. I never thought about it that way," Ananya admitted.

Types of Habits

"We all have habits that we use daily. These habits can be classified into three types.

- The first category includes habits that we simply don't catch sight of because they have been a part of our lives for as long as we can remember, such as tying shoelaces or brushing our teeth.

- The second category includes healthy habits that we work hard to establish, such as exercising, choosing a healthy diet, or sleeping enough.

- The last category of habits is like walking on thin ice, not good for us like overspending, procrastinating, or being remiss about things," Sivaranjan explained.

"So, habits can be good or bad, and we all have a mix of them," Ananya summarized.

"True. We as humans carry a web of all categories of habits. According to Duke University researchers, habits determine more than 40% of what we do rather than decisions. This implies that we can change a significant portion of our lives simply by eliminating bad habits and replacing them with good ones," Sivaranjan added.

"That's quite empowering to know," Vaibhav said.

"People who fully comprehend this have discovered wonderful new ways to improve their lives. You look up any successful figure, and you will discover that they follow a routine or a set of productive habits to stay ahead of the curve," Sivaranjan stated.

"It sounds like building the right habits is crucial for success," Ananya noted.

"Absolutely. Now, let's understand why all the successful people in the world emphasize more on building habits," Sivaranjan continued.

The Power of Habits

"We are all aware that developing habits takes time and effort. You'll need a strategy, accountability, commitment, grit, patience, and other qualities to succeed, and you'll face challenges like laziness, procrastination, and overwhelm. As a result, it's no surprise that many people give up too soon, while the rest don't even realize they're doing it," Sivaranjan said.

"That sounds challenging. So, what's in it for me if I cultivate good habits?" Vaibhav asked.

"Aside from feeling accomplished, cultivating self-discipline, and being more intentional about your thoughts and actions, here are five payoffs to developing and sticking to the right habits," Sivaranjan stated.

"Okay, let's hear them," Ananya replied.

Pick the right habit and reach your goals

As Jim Rohn said, 'Motivation is what gets you started; habit is what keeps you going.' Whether it is about starting a business, writing a bestselling book, building a dream house, or being a successful professional. The right habits come into play as they are consistent, automated, and less challenging once you keep following them," Sivaranjan explained.

"Habits can make the path to big goals more manageable," Vaibhav agreed.

Take your pick on the right habits and meet your higher self

"Consider all of the successful business owners, writers, and CEOs you know. They show up day in and day out even when they aren't inspired, when they face challenges, or when they simply don't 'feel like it,'" Sivaranjan continued.

"So, habits help them stay on track even during tough times," Ananya noted.

Picking the right habits means sticking with the right people

"Benjamin Franklin said, 'Your net worth to the world is usually determined by what remains after your bad habits are subtracted from your good ones.'" Sivaranjan quoted.

Sticking with the right people eventually makes you think, act, and pick their habits. You may like the way they talk, present themselves, or their ingrained values. The way someone else inspires you and compels you to be like them, there's no denying that what you do regularly (aka your habits) has an impact on those around you. Developing good habits is thus a sure-fire way to help or affect others and, more importantly, to set a benchmark for the people in your circle.

"That's true. Being around the right people can influence us positively," Ananya remarked.

Pick the right habits and enrich the quality of your life

"Certain habits, known as keystone habits, have the potential to influence multiple aspects of your life. Take exercise for example, which not only improves your health and fitness but also your productivity, time management, energy management, and mental health," Sivaranjan elaborated.

"Furthermore, two or more habits combine to form routines—morning routines, evening routines, Sunday night routines, and end-of-workday routines— and it is these routines that help us be more efficient and effective, allowing us to have highly productive days consistently, " Sivaranjan said.

"I see how interconnected our habits can be," Vaibhav noted.

Pick the right habits and stay consistent

Your talent may or may not give you success, but your disciplined efforts will help you reach your desired future," Sivaranjan said.

Pick the right habits and reap lifelong benefits

With all of the preceding advantages, these will not be one-time occurrences due to habit. Because habits are any activity that you do regularly, you can continue:

- achieving goal after goal,

- being the person, you aspire to be,

- assisting those around you, and

- improving your overall quality of life

You'll feel more accomplished, develop self-discipline, and be more intentional, and thanks to the right set of habits, you'll reap these benefits for years to come," Sivaranjan concluded.

"Wow, I never paid much heed to my habits till now. This is eye-opening," Vaibhav admitted. "Now I know what I have to do to stay in the game," he continued.

"Most of us focus on the end goals and the final achievements, but we often neglect the importance of how we begin. The start of any journey, project, or habit sets the foundation for success. If we optimize our starting steps, by planning carefully and establishing strong initial routines, we set ourselves up for a smoother and more successful path toward our goals," Sivaranjan shared the nuggets of wisdom with Vaibhav and Ananya.

"That's really insightful. I've been struggling to stick to a study routine. I think this will help," Ananya said.

"Me too. I often find myself procrastinating on assignments and then cramming at the last minute," Vaibhav added.

Vaibhav, understanding what his uncle just shared, then asked, "I would like to know how to form new habits that will get me through my future endeavors."

"Yes, that will surely help us," said Ananya.

"Well, let us get going then!" nodded Sivaranjan.

What does it take to Form a Habit?

"Our habits influence our lives. According to research, repetition drives roughly half of our daily actions. This is most likely why behavioral scientists and psychologists have spent so much time researching how to develop and maintain positive habits. Regular sleep and exercise, a healthy diet, an organized schedule, and mindfulness are just a few examples of practices that can improve our work, relationships, and mental health if done regularly," explained Sivaranjan.

"What if those things aren't second nature to you? What is required to form a new habit?" asked Vaibhav.

"Habits are automatic behaviors that our brains have wired into them through repetition. We perform these behaviors less consciously as time passes. Charles Duhigg describes the Habit Loop in his book *The Power of Habit.*

Each habit's outcome is stored in our brains. If the feedback is positive, the brain will respond automatically the next time the cue appears. As a result, the Habit

Loop is formed, and the neural pathway for the habit is hardwired into our brains," quoted Sivaranjan.

"How long does it take for a habit to be formed?" Ananya asked.

"The entire habit-forming process only takes two to three weeks (14 to 21 days). And once a neural pathway for a habit has been established in our brain, it is permanent," Sivaranjan replied.

"According to studies, if people are in the same environment, they will perform automated, unconscious behaviors the same way every time. Because all of the familiar cues and rewards are no longer present, changes in our routine or taking a vacation can be beneficial in breaking habits," explained Sivaranjan.

"That means I should know what habit I need to inculcate in my life, then set a routine to establish its existence and follow that routine to get the reward," Ananya enquired.

"Yes, this is exactly what it takes to get into gears," Sivaranjan muffled.

"Fair enough, now that I know what it takes to form a habit, Uncle, please walk me through the holy grail of forming productive habits," Vaibhav requested.

Ananya added, "I'm curious too. I've struggled with sticking to good habits in college. I want to know how to make these habits stick."

"Yes, let's dive in!" said Sivaranjan.

Ways to Form Productive Habits

Make a list of habits you want to develop in the long run

"Sit in a quiet place, and think about your priorities, your short-term and long-term goals, and what you would need to achieve them.

- Have an upper hand in your work.

- Ace the race of reaching the ladder.

- Improve your relationships at the workplace.

- Be the reason people believe in humanity.

The best place to start is to review the common productive habits of successful entrepreneurs or leaders. Then incorporate those practices into your daily chores. Believe me, Vaibhav, repetition is the key to your leading light," said Sivaranjan pressingly.

Ananya nodded, "I think making a list will help me stay focused. I often get distracted by social events or just feel overwhelmed by everything."

Take note of the habits that do not serve you

"Recognize the existence of a bad habit and then zero in on the specific behavior that needs to change," Sivaranjan explained. "Some people struggle with this, especially if the habit is unconscious. Here are a few pointers:

- Ask others for feedback on your behaviors in specific situations, or if they've noticed any habits, you're not aware of.

- Look for patterns in your behavior and pay attention to the routines you tend to follow at work.

- Examine your thought processes as well as your gut reaction to specific situations.

- Examine how you complete tasks, manage others, and collaborate in groups.

Going through this exercise allows you to push back and avoid having your brain's auto-pilot kick in."

"So, it's about being aware of what I'm doing and why," Vaibhav nodded.

Ananya agreed, "I've noticed that I tend to procrastinate on assignments until the last minute. I need to identify what triggers that behavior."

Read between the lines and create connections between cues

"Identifying the habit is all about getting to the bottom of the issue. You want to know what causes you to engage in an unwanted habit so you can disrupt that relationship and, eventually, break the habit," Sivaranjan explained.

"Work backward to determine what acts as a trigger. Slow down when you notice yourself engaging in negative behavior and use your awareness as a signal to ask yourself: What is going on with me emotionally, mentally, physically, or socially right now?

Remove physical triggers as soon as possible. Don't, for example, leave a distracting cell phone on your desk. Put it away so you're not tempted to text or browse social media whenever you're feeling overwhelmed with work."

"Got it. So, remove triggers and be more self-aware," Vaibhav summarized.

Ananya added, "I often find myself checking my phone during study sessions. I need to start putting it away."

Always keep a "Plan B" lock and load

"Now that you're aware of your habits and what causes them, you can confront and deal with them directly," Sivaranjan elaborated. ***Breaking a habit does not always require stopping action; however, substituting it for something healthier or more desirable.*** When presented with a cue, consider what else you can do to improve the outcome. Instead of automatically complaining to a coworker when you're stressed or angry, try a few minutes of deep breathing to relax."

"That's a good idea. I should have alternatives ready," Vaibhav agreed.

Ananya nodded, "I can try going for a walk instead of scrolling through my phone when I need a break from work."

Follow the cues for encouragement

"Consider prompts to be the positive cues. These are reminders to keep you on track with desired behaviors and to assist you in breaking any bad habits you may have," Sivaranjan explained. "Set up an alert on your computer to complete a task 30 minutes before the end of each workday, for example, if you have trouble remembering to respond to emails each day."

"Okay, I'll set up reminders for important tasks," Vaibhav noted.

Perseverance above all

"Remember the two to three weeks it takes to form a habit? Breaking a habit, on the other hand, takes at least the same amount of time," Sivaranjan said. "New brain connections must form, old brain firings must calm down, and new patterns must take time to replace the old. Don't punish yourself for mistakes, or use them as justifications for quitting and reverting to bad habits. Take a breather! Take things one day at a time, keep your eyes glued on the prize, and keep dreaming Vaibhav, it will take you to good places in life."

"I will, uncle," Vaibhav smiled.

Ananya smiled too, "I'll keep that in mind. It's reassuring to know that it's normal to slip up sometimes."

"As we move forward into the uncertain future of work, we can expect more context shifts to disrupt existing work habits. While this may appear daunting to organizations, it creates opportunities to assist employees in developing new, positive habits at work," Sivaranjan continued. "On the personal front, it takes time to change behavior, so be patient and don't be concerned about slip-ups. However, once you've instilled good habits in yourself, and kept any troublesome habits in check, your workplace will benefit significantly."

"Amazing! I am stunned by the role of habits in our lives; they can make or break us. From now on, I will keep a tab on my habits and work on improving or banishing them, as per their place in my life," shrieked Vaibhav.

"I am so glad to share the wisdom with you both, Vaibhav and Ananya, and proud to see you grow through these lessons of professionalism. It certainly is leaving its mark on you," exclaimed Sivaranjan.

Vaibhav hugged his uncle and thanked him for helping him establish his first step in the professional world.

Ananya smiled warmly and shook Sivaranjan's hand, saying, "Thank you, Uncle. Your guidance means a lot to me. I'm excited to start applying these lessons and building better habits."

Teamwork
Wins
Championships

Chapter 10

Teamwork - Less Me and More We

Let's go the distance and uncover something compelling today with a story, said Sivaranjan.

A company held an event for around 35 employees. They were a team of enthusiastic, bright, and dedicated employees. However, the only problem was that this team did not share information or anything among themselves. The manager felt that they were too focused on working in silos instead of as a team.

"Is that a common issue in many organizations?" Vaibhav asked. "Do people often get so engrossed in their tasks that they forget the importance of collaboration?"

"Yes, Vaibhav, working in silos can bring up a scenario like this," Sivaranjan nodded.

"So, the manager came up with a fun activity to teach them the importance of collaboration and teamwork. They all were asked to gather in the cafeteria where all the chairs and tables were stacked and kept away. All they could see there were hundreds of different colored balloons. They had no idea about the activity; however, they were pumped to participate and have fun."

"That sounds intriguing!" Ananya exclaimed. "What was the activity about?"

"There was a box of balloons in the center of the room, and the manager asked each of the employees to pick one up, blow it, and write their name on it. Within minutes the room was filled with balloons with the names on them. Now the manager scattered all the balloons to mix them."

"Interesting. What happened next?" Vaibhav leaned in, curious.

"The team was instructed to find the balloons with their names on them, and they had only fifteen minutes to find them. If the balloons popped, the ones with their names on them would be disqualified. The team had to be careful and quick to find the one with their name on it. The room was filled with chaos, shouts, and pops. The fifteen minutes were over and none of them was able to find their balloon."

"Wow! That must have been frustrating for them," Ananya said.

"It was," Sivaranjan continued. "Then the manager instructed the team members to find a balloon with a name on it and give it to the person whose name was on it. Within a few minutes, each member of the team had a balloon with their name on it."

"That's a brilliant way to illustrate teamwork!" Vaibhav said, impressed.

"It is," Sivaranjan agreed. "The manager then said, *'We are much more efficient when we are willing to share. And we are better problem solvers when we work together rather than individually.'*"

"Teamwork can simply work and amplify the productivity of the work," Sivaranjan added. "Every organization has shared goals and objectives, and it takes more than one employee to work in a symphony to achieve them."

"Let's understand the nitty-gritty of teamwork," said Sivaranjan.

What is Teamwork?

"When a group of people works cooperatively and efficiently toward a common goal or to achieve a specific goal, this is referred to as teamwork. A work environment that values teamwork encourages employees to develop trust in their colleagues and to maintain professional integrity. The positive climate created by collaboration fosters strong bonds among employees and capitalizes on their unique talents."

"Working collaboratively with others to develop your interpersonal skills can prepare you for future leadership roles or even help you transition to another field," Sivaranjan explained. "Teamwork can also be advantageous by:

Aligning team members: As team members get to know one another, they establish supportive bonds that help them align their goals and motivate them to work harder to support one another.

Bringing different perspectives to the table: It allows teams to use problem-solving skills and consider various angles to make more informed decisions. Appreciate others' points of view.

Providing prompt feedback: Team members can share ideas, inform each other's actions, benefit from different skills, and use each other's expertise to adjust actions and provide more consistent output.

Improving productivity: A team can boost productivity by reducing the overall shared workload, pressure, and accountability on an individual.

Supporting professional development: Team members learn from one another as they collaborate. They appreciate each other's contributions and can put their strengths to use while developing their underdeveloped skills with the help of others."

"According to studies," Sivaranjan continued, "organizations that emphasize teamwork innovate and spot mistakes faster, find better solutions to problems, and achieve higher productivity."

"Interdependence is one of the many principles that build cooperation and collaboration in an organization," Vaibhav noted.

"Yes, Vaibhav," Sivaranjan agreed. "In an interdependent work environment, somebody's input is your output and your input becomes someone's output, more like working together and making headway toward the shared goals."

"For example," Ananya added, "if we look up cricket or football, working together as a team contributes to winning the game. When there are so many players on the team, a robust sense of collaboration and coordination matters the most."

"Absolutely," Sivaranjan said. "Being a part of a team in the office demands you to know your peers and be 100% invested in the overall success of the organization."

"Working together boosts productivity and performance, and it requires you to lean on your team for motivation and support all along," Sivaranjan emphasized. "Salespeople, for example, thrive on healthy competition, but they close more deals and benefit the organization when they work as a team."

"For our projects in college," Vaibhav recalled, "our professors used to divide us into teams. We used to brainstorm together and reach a conclusion as a team. It made us think quickly, implement ideas significantly, and present our projects more extensively. Also, it was fun to work together and gather different perspectives and ideas."

"I had a similar experience," Ananya chimed in. "In one of our major projects, we had to develop a business plan. Each of us brought different skills to the table— some were good with numbers, others with presentation, and some with the creative aspects. By working together, we created a plan that was much better than what any of us could have done alone."

"Yes, the beauty of working together is that you have others (your team) on your side," smiled Sivaranjan.

"Shall we put down roots to the grounds that make us work together?" asked Sivaranjan.

"Sure, uncle, let's dig in!" said Vaibhav and Ananya together.

Payoffs of Teamwork in the Workplace

Do you remember the Border-Gavaskar Trophy 2020-21? - asked Sivaranjan

"Oh, that match! It was the epic series win; I was at the edge of my chair the entire time," said Vaibhav.

"Yes, Team India, despite a slew of injuries and the absence of talismanic captain Virat Kohli, defeated Australia for the second time in two years in a Test series to retain the high-profile Border-Gavaskar Trophy," Sivaranjan recounted.

"The Indian cricket team, led by Ajinkya Rahane, defeated the Australian team by three wickets in the fourth and final Test in Brisbane to win the four-match series 2-1. As a result, India made history by becoming the first team to defeat Australia at The Gabba in 32 years."

"The then Indian Prime Minister Narendra Modi praised the team's 'brilliant team spirit' and 'hard work' in Australia, which enabled them to 'gloriously' win the series," Sivaranjan continued. "We got good news from the cricket field this month. After some hiccups, the Indian team bounced back magnificently and won the series in Australia. The hard work and teamwork of our team were inspiring,' the Indian PM Modi said in 'Mann Ki Baat.'"

"When the people in a team understand each other, their responsibilities, and firmly decide to play their part, nothing can stop them from succeeding. Working together as a team creates a perfect synergy to make anything possible," Sivaranjan said.

"Absolutely, uncle," Ananya added, her eyes lighting up with enthusiasm. "I remember watching that series and being amazed at how each player stepped up, especially when key players were injured. It wasn't just about individual performances but how they supported each other, both on and off the field. It really showed the strength of their teamwork."

"That's a great point, Ananya," Vaibhav agreed. "In cricket, just like in any team, everyone has to understand their role and be ready to back up their teammates. It's not just about scoring runs or taking wickets individually but about working together to win matches."

"Exactly," Sivaranjan agreed. "Whether it's cricket or any other field, when team members trust and support each other, they can achieve extraordinary things. It's the collective effort that leads to success, not just individual brilliance."

Ananya nodded. "And the camaraderie they displayed, even in tough times, was so inspiring. It shows that when you have a strong team spirit and everyone is working towards a common goal, you can overcome any obstacle."

Let's find out how working together sprouts success.

It increases work efficiency

Sivaranjan stated, "According to statistics, employees who work as a team complete tasks much faster and more efficiently than those who work alone. Working on different assignments as a team reduces workloads for all employees by sharing ideas and responsibilities."

It enhances learning opportunities

Sivaranjan continued, "Employees in an organization vary in terms of their work experience, expertise, and skills. Collaboration allows these employees to interact with one another while working on a project. This interaction is a great learning opportunity for new employees because they can learn skills from more experienced employees that they did not have before."

It Brings Out Fresh Ideas

"Did you know that teams with diverse backgrounds— whether it's gender, age, or ethnicity—are significantly more creative and perform better?" Sivaranjan began. "According to a McKinsey study, such teams can perform up to 35% better."

"That's impressive, uncle," Vaibhav replied. "So diversity really makes a difference?"

"Absolutely. When you have a mix of perspectives, you can see the big picture more clearly. This diversity leads to an exponential increase in the number of new ideas," Sivaranjan explained. "When people work alone, their motivation to innovate can decrease. But in a team, the sense of collaboration and accountability drives everyone to consistently deliver their best work."

Peer Recognition Makes Team Members Go the Extra Mile

"Receiving appreciation from your co-workers is critical in the workplace," Sivaranjan continued. "We often underestimate how effective it is in engaging employees."

"Understood," Ananya said. "Feeling valued by your peers must be a huge motivator."

"It is. Without peer connection, an individual working alone might feel demotivated and underappreciated. But when you receive proper respect and recognition from your co-workers, it significantly boosts your motivation to go the extra mile," Sivaranjan elaborated.

Group Cohesion

"Group cohesion is crucial for the success of any business," Sivaranjan emphasized. "If individuals focus solely on their own benefit, rather than the company's, it can be detrimental."

"I can see how that would lead to problems," Vaibhav said thoughtfully. "If everyone has different goals, the project and the business could suffer."

"Right. When everyone is aligned and working toward the same goals, the team and the business thrives," Sivaranjan pointed out. *"Teamwork is the bonding agent that brings people together and encourages them to rely on one another. It makes progress smoother and helps team members overcome obstacles."*

This reminds me of a time," Ananya shared, "when we had a group assignment that seemed impossible to complete in the given timeframe. But by dividing tasks based on each person's strengths and supporting each other, we not only finished on time but also received the highest grade in the class."

"That's a great example, Ananya," Sivaranjan said. "It shows how collective effort and mutual support can turn challenging situations into successes."

"Always remember," Sivaranjan said, *"There are no winners in a losing team and no losers in a winning team.* Teamwork is like creating a spark of fire—it takes two flints to make fire. If you keep the spirit of teamwork alive, you will always find your way to success."

"I understand, uncle," Vaibhav responded.

"I can see how essential teamwork is for achieving success," added Ananya.

"That's right," Sivaranjan concluded. "Embrace the power of teamwork, and you'll not only succeed but also help others succeed along the way."

Decode

Reconnect

Align

Chapter 11

People Reading Skills

"Professionalism encompasses a set of skills, attitudes, and behaviors that are deemed appropriate in the workplace. It is often characterized by expertise, competence, a strong work ethic, and a commitment to continuous learning and development," Sivaranjan explained. "Additionally, professionalism may include qualities such as reliability, responsibility, good communication, and ethical behavior. In many fields, a code of conduct or professional standards is in place to guide behavior and ensure a level of professionalism is upheld."

This is the reason Vaibhav and Ananya, we are deep diving into different topics because professionalism is infused with more than one thing in particular, added Sivaranjan.

"Uncle, I understand professionalism, now that you have made it such a sublime experience for me," Vaibhav agreed.

"Fair enough. Shall we take the lead to the next on our list? Vaibhav, have you ever looked at someone and thought you knew everything about them just by looking at them? Were you correct? Or did you misjudge some aspect of their personality?"

"Sometimes I feel like I can understand people, however, I'm not always right," Vaibhav admitted.

"Ananya, what about you? Have you ever felt that you could read someone just by observing them?"

"Absolutely, Uncle. There have been times when I thought I had someone figured out, however, later I realized I was way off," Ananya shared.

"Whether you were right about them or not, you just attempted to understand someone, which is a skill that many of us would like to have. After all, if you can tell when your boss is happy, you'll know when to ask for a raise. When you know your parents are upset, it's not the time to tell them you scratched their car. It all comes down to understanding what reading people entails and how it works."

Judith Orloff MD, the NY Times bestselling author of *The Empath's Survival Guide: Life Strategies for Sensitive People, Thriving as an Empath, and Emotional Freedom* writes in *Psychology Today*:

"Logic alone will not tell you the whole story about anybody. You must surrender to other forms of vital information to learn to read the important nonverbal intuitive cues that people give off. To see someone clearly, you must remain objective and receive information neutrally without distorting it."

"Uncle, that makes a lot of sense. I can see how reading the cues can help me become a strong leader in my journey as a professional," Vaibhav noted.

"Absolutely, Vaibhav. It's all about understanding people on a deeper level," Ananya added. "I've noticed that sometimes people have unspoken expectations, and being able to read those can really make a difference in how you interact with them."

"So, with that note, let's dive into understanding the skill of reading people's minds at the workplace," Sivaranjan suggested.

Why is it Important to Understand People?

"Vaibhav, Ananya, have you ever thought why am I emphasizing working on the skill of reading people? Why do you even bother with it?" Sivaranjan asked.

"Honestly, I haven't given it much thought. But I guess it can be useful in many situations," Vaibhav responded.

"There are a variety of reasons why this can be a useful skill. First and foremost, it instructs you on how to approach someone. If they appear friendly, you may be more inclined to approach them with a friendly smile and greeting. If they appear unhappy, you are more likely to approach them with a reason rather than simply saying hello. Understanding how they feel just by looking at them can help you anticipate whatever is going on, and the better you get at it, the better you'll be at talking to people," Sivaranjan explained.

"That sounds quite useful. I can see how misjudging someone's emotions could lead to misunderstandings," Ananya reflected.

"If you don't know how to understand people, you may end up misinterpreting something they do, an action, or a facial expression, and you may begin to make wrong assumptions about them. Maybe you see their face and think they're angry when they're just upset about something. You might think they're unfriendly, but they're just frustrated with something going on around them. You will be able to advance your life in a variety of ways by improving your people reading skills," Sivaranjan elaborated.

"Reading people can help you figure out whom to approach with your great new idea (and when to approach them) and whom to avoid. It also tells you how to introduce something to them, whether from a factual or more fun and creative standpoint."

"Uncle, it sounds like reading people is a skill that becomes second nature with practice," Vaibhav observed.

"Yes, it does, Vaibhav. If you practice reading people often enough, it will become second nature to you. What's more, you've probably been doing it your entire life without even realizing. That's because it's something that even children will experiment with, without realizing the magnitude of its importance," Sivaranjan confirmed.

How to Appreciate People are Different not Difficult

"Uncle, how can I become better at reading people?" Vaibhav asked eagerly.

"Reading people's minds does not require superpowers. Indeed, one executive believes that getting a good read on people is critical to advancing in your career," Sivaranjan replied. "Loren Miner, COO of recruitment services company Decision Toolbox, has become 'an expert on reading minds.' She says, 'It's all about perception for her. Being perceptive leads to greater success in life and business. Perception differences may be a deal's greatest vulnerability.'"

"Could you share some insights to help understand people-reading skills better?" Ananya requested.

"Certainly. Miner provided some pointers to help anyone improve their people-reading skills."

Be a better listener

'You have to go in with big ears and a small mouth,' says Miner. 'If you don't, you'll miss the subtle cues that people give.' Her strategy is to start an open-ended conversation, which sparks a good conversation and allows her to listen to the other person. 'You can hear an engaged and passionate voice so easily,' she says," Sivaranjan shared.

"Listening more and talking less, got it," Vaibhav noted.

Be humble and understand the person's preferences and background

'Everyone approaches any situation with a unique set of lens based on their experiences and culture,' Miner says. Consider who you're dealing with before any meeting and try to create an environment that fits their comfort zone." Millennials, for example, maybe less comfortable in face-to-face meetings and more familiar with video calls. Generation Jones, on the other hand, thrives and may prefer face-to-face interactions," Sivaranjan continued.

"That makes sense. Different people have different comfort zones," Ananya acknowledged.

Take note of the nonverbal cues

"The most important skill for employees to have is awareness. Picking up on someone's body language, whether it's poor eye contact, bad posture, crossed arms, or something else, may appear simple and obvious, but Miner says it's very easy to overlook. Top performers are frequently emotionally intelligent and perceptive," Sivaranjan added.

"I'll pay more attention to nonverbal cues from now on," Vaibhav promised.

Learn and accept different personality types

"Understanding different personality types is one of the most important aspects of reading people. *Personality analysis helps them understand people and how they differ from one another.* Different strategies can provide you with the necessary knowledge and insight into how to understand others. It eventually assists you in establishing a foundation level from which to move forward," Sivaranjan concluded.

Ananya added, "I remember in one of our group assignments, we had to understand each other's strengths and weaknesses to work effectively. Knowing different personality types would've been really helpful."

"When it comes to understanding different personalities, Vaibhav and Ananya, we have to decode human behavior. Let's explore it in detail," said Sivaranjan while Vaibhav and Ananya were jotting it down.

How to Understand Different Personality Traits?

"Vaibhav, Ananya, have you ever said the same thing to two people and garnered two completely different responses?" Sivaranjan asked.

"Yes, it happens all the time. It's interesting how different people react differently to the same thing," Vaibhav replied.

"Absolutely," Ananya agreed. "I've seen that some people take feedback really well, while others get defensive."

"Based on their personality style, each person 'hear' you differently! You say the same thing, however, they 'hear' something different. Different is not a bad thing; it is simply different! A lack of understanding of oneself and others can result in serious issues such as tension, disappointment, hurt feelings, unmet expectations, and poor communication. As you are aware, working with a problem is difficult, especially when you do not understand what is going on inside the mind of another person," Sivaranjan explained.

"Uncle, it seems like understanding different personalities is key to better communication and teamwork," Vaibhav remarked.

"Precisely. Every individual has a unique perspective and it makes them who they are. Some may call it personality, while others name it temperament. Let us understand people through the lens of the theory of human emotion." Sivaranjan affirmed.

Theory of Human Emotions

"When engaging with people in any setting, it's normal to consider their skill set, such as expertise in sales, IT, marketing, or leadership. However, Harvard Business Review (HBR) suggests that understanding the mix of personality traits is also vital. This awareness does not come by itself. Even a group made up solely of IT specialists may have disparate personalities and points of view."

"According to HBR, good teams include a mix of personality types. Let me explain these types to you," Sivaranjan continued.

1. Driver

"This personality type focuses on end results and making progress towards the attainment of the goals. They are confident and assertive, which allows them to take charge of situations and make decisions quickly. They tend to be natural leaders who can motivate and push their fellow members to work towards achieving their objectives," Sivaranjan elaborated.

"That sounds like a valuable trait, but I can see how it could lead to conflicts if not managed properly," Vaibhav noted.

Ananya asked, "Uncle, do people with strong leadership traits clash with others who have different working styles?"

"Yes, drivers are highly focused on their goals, which sometimes makes it challenging for them to prioritize listening to others and are usually impatient. If something is not going as per their plans or others aren't performing in the way they would like, they become agitated easily. This instance gives rise to a conflict situation within the team, if not managed properly," Sivaranjan agreed.

2. Analytical

"This category gives keen attention to details, emphasizes facts and data, and is highly logical, which makes them great problem-solvers. Being data enthusiasts, they're skilled in breaking down complex problems into smaller, more manageable parts, which enables them to stay organized. Because of their focus on detail and data, analytical individuals are great at identifying potential obstacles or risks and finding potential solutions," Sivaranjan explained.

"Their careful nature would be beneficial in fields like engineering or finance," Vaibhav observed.

Ananya nodded, "We all need someone analytical in our teams and groups for troubleshooting and ensuring everything works perfectly."

"However, analytical individuals play safe while making decisions. They prefer to accumulate a bundle of information before making a decision. Until they're confident in their analysis, they hesitate to take quick decisions or risks. This makes them valuable members of a team, particularly in fields like engineering, finance, or data analysis," Sivaranjan continued.

"Being so focused on facts and data might have its downside," Ananya noted.

"Probably. People having analytical personalities face difficulty in communication and building interpersonal relationships. Because they tend to be very focused on facts and data, they may overlook the emotional or personal aspects of a situation. They may also struggle to explain their reasoning to others who may not have the same level of technical expertise or understanding of the subject matter. It's important for Analytical individuals to work on developing strong communication skills and building strong relationships with their team members in order to be effective in a team setting," Sivaranjan explained.

3. Amiable

"Individuals having an amiable personality type are friendly in nature and focus on building relationships, which enables them to socialize easily. They tend to be warm, empathetic, approachable, and most importantly, they're good at putting others at ease. ***Amiable individuals are also highly empathetic and are often able to pick up on others' emotions and respond in a supportive way.*** This makes an amiable person perform well in creating a positive team environment," Sivaranjan explained.

"That sounds like a great quality to have in a team. But are there any challenges?" Vaibhav asked.

Ananya added, "If I understand correctly, amiable people often keep their spirits high, however, sometimes they avoid tough conversations to keep happy, don't they, Uncle?"

"Yes, this personality type usually faces difficulty in setting boundaries, which sometimes puts them into tricky situations. For instance, to maintain positive relationships, they may not speak up when they disagree with others. Therefore, it's important for Amiable individuals to work on developing their assertiveness skills and setting clear boundaries in order to be effective in a team setting. Despite these challenges, Amiable individuals bring many valuable skills and strengths to a team. Their focus on relationships and empathy can help create a supportive and positive team environment, and their conflict-resolution skills can be invaluable in navigating disagreements and finding solutions that work for everyone," Sivaranjan clarified.

4. Expressive

"This personality type is highly creative, enthusiastic, charismatic, and loves being the centre of attention. Expressive individuals are highly skilled at thinking outside the box and generating new ideas. They also possess the knack for inspiring others and owing to their creativity and enthusiasm, they build excitement around a project," Sivaranjan shared.

"Wow, they sound like a lot of fun to work with," Vaibhav remarked.

"They can be. People having expressive personalities possess excellent communication skills, which enables them to present their ideas in a compelling way and get others on board with their ideas. Being focused on the bigger picture, they sometimes face difficulty in giving attention to details that are necessary for successful implementation. It's important for Expressive individuals to work on developing their organizational and time-management skills in order to be effective in a team setting. They may also benefit from working with individuals who are highly detail-oriented and can help ensure that tasks are completed accurately and thoroughly. Despite these challenges, expressive individuals bring many valuable skills and strengths to a team. Their focus on creativity and enthusiasm can help generate new and innovative ideas, and their ability to inspire and engage others can be invaluable in building a strong and motivated team," Sivaranjan said.

"Knowing people for who they are can be challenging. Even more complicated is the fact that you must accept them for who they are. ***Picking up on their signals and understanding them on a deeper level will allow you to aspire greatness in them.*** You can compel them to act and perform well in their roles. It assists you in developing an understanding of them and heading towards success as a team. And it is their success that will account for your own. You take the initiative as an individual and as a group. You can only do that if you've honed your reading skills," explained Sivaranjan.

"Uncle, I understand the influence of people's reading skills and that I will inculcate the practice of reading people in my life from now on," Vaibhav said while finishing his notes.

"I'll definitely be more attentive to these aspects too," Ananya added, smiling as she closed her notebook.

Sivaranjan smiled at the gesture.

Be a Good Listener

Encourage other to talk about themselves

Chapter 12

Interpersonal Relationships

"Vaibhav, I am sure you might be fond of cricket," Sivaranjan asked with a knowing smile.

Vaibhav jumped with excitement before replying, "Yes, absolutely!" He grinned widely, anticipating an enjoyable conversation about the sport.

Turning to Ananya, Sivaranjan continued, "Ananya, how about you? Are you interested in cricket?"

Ananya nodded, "Yes, I follow cricket casually. It's quite popular, so it's hard not to be aware of what's happening."

Sivaranjan nodded, acknowledging both their interests. "Great to know. Do you remember the Champions Trophy 2017? When the Indian cricket team was competing in the Champions Trophy that year, things were not going well behind the scenes between Virat Kohli and Anil Kumble. They reached the finals but had to face a big defeat by Pakistan."

"Yes, I remember that," Vaibhav said thoughtfully. "The media kept talking about the tension between them."

"Critics did not stop asking if India had to suffer as a result of the strained relationship between the coach and the captain," Sivaranjan explained. "It was certainly not the only reason for India's failure in the finals, but we all know that a team's morale and spirit are heavily influenced by the interpersonal relationships among its members. Our corporate lives and the success of an organization are quite alike."

"People who work together should emphasize bonding well with their team to perform at their best," Ananya added. "Individuals must be honest with one another to maintain healthy interpersonal dynamics and, ultimately, a positive work environment."

"One thing that balances everything else in a workplace is our interpersonal relationships with our colleagues or co-workers. Interpersonal relationships are equally significant in today's workplace. Results are unavoidable in an organization where there is a top-down demonstration of a 'one team' approach from the leadership level to the nth level of the institution. Failures or challenges will always be a part of the journey, however, if the entire team works toward one goal and one objective while maintaining good interpersonal relationships and understanding among key stakeholders, it is a completely different story. Work culture and values are important to progressive and modern-day organizations."

"Now, if we take care of our interpersonal relationships, we can emerge positively at work, enhance emotional intelligence, and perform well at any level. Let's understand interpersonal relationships better," said Sivaranjan.

What are Interpersonal Relationships?

"The fundamental concept of an interpersonal relationship is a strong bond between two or more people. Workplace interpersonal relationships are important for both job success and career advancement. Employees will be able to communicate and understand each other more effectively if they have positive interpersonal relationships," Sivaranjan explained.

"Any of the following can form an interpersonal relationship within or outside of the workplace:

Individuals who work in the same organization

People who work on the same team

Relationships with customers

Office colleagues'/friends' relationship

Relationships with people other than professionals (for example, the servicemen, etc.)

See, the relationship you might have built with your friends at college or with the individuals you worked on projects with as a team, is an example of interpersonal relationships. When you all studied together for those four years, you participated in competitions together,0 worked as a team, and made quite a few friends for life. Somehow you ended up knowing them better while spending time together; this is how we build on our interpersonal relationships and excel together at the end of the day," explained Sivaranjan.

"Wow, it's an amazing approach to doing better as a team member," Vaibhav nodded his head in agreement.

"Absolutely," Ananya added.

How to Develop Interpersonal Relationships

"An individual spends approximately seven to eight hours per day at work, and it is practically impossible for him to work alone. At work, one needs people to talk to and discuss various issues. *According to research, working in groups increases productivity significantly more than working alone. It also allows them to know each other better to create a healthy ambiance in the workplace.*"

"Let's look into various ways to improve interpersonal relationships when you enter the corporate world."

Take Initiative: Increase your interaction with co-workers

"Discussions must take place on an open platform where everyone is free to express their thoughts and opinions. Written communication is one of the most effective modes of communication in the workplace. Make your emails self-explanatory and include a cc to all relevant employees. Ignoring any of your co-workers may cause him harm and jeopardize your relationship with the individual in question. Avoid keeping things from your co-workers."

"Ananya, have you noticed how including everyone in group emails or chats makes a difference?" Sivaranjan asked.

"Yes, it creates a sense of belonging and transparency," Ananya replied. "In my internship, our team lead always made sure to keep everyone in the loop, and it made us feel more connected and valued."

Stay true to your word

"When you say what you do and do what you say, it becomes easier for people to put their faith in your words. Word patterns are powerful creative forces. They express our reality. They broadcast our hopes and dreams to the entire world. Our agreements are defined by them. They are also the foundation of personal integrity. Every time we speak, we follow some sort of path. The quality of that road, as well as its length, will be directly proportional to how well we maintain our integrity through our word and language choices."

"I had a friend who always kept his promises. It made working with him very reliable and trustworthy," Vaibhav shared.

Meet your deadlines

"If you commit to completing work in the stipulated time, then stick to your timeline. You must know the value of your words. Setting and meeting deadlines regularly can boost your and your team's morale. Knowing you can set a clear timetable for your outstanding tasks and complete them on time can boost your confidence and self-esteem. As time is the most precious asset, respect it, and people will respect you."

"During our final year project, we had strict deadlines," Ananya said. "It was stressful, but meeting those deadlines as a team was incredibly satisfying and boosted our confidence."

Take a spoonful of respect with colleagues

"Respect for those around you will effectively foster good relationships and create an ideal work environment. Lack of respect in the workplace can lead to misunderstandings and chaos. Be courteous and gracious and help improve the work of others. Have an ear for suggestions, feedback, and recommendations."

"Respect is key," Vaibhav agreed. "I've seen projects fail because team members didn't respect each other's ideas or contributions."

Practice self-awareness

"Self-awareness refers to a person's ability to recognize what they are feeling and why they are feeling it. Self-awareness is one of four components of emotional intelligence, according to psychologists: empathy, emotions, and relationship building. Being aware of your emotions and feelings will assist you in understanding the information conveyed to others. Lack of self-awareness can have negative consequences in the workplace, resulting in lower productivity levels."

"I've found that understanding my emotions helps me communicate better with people around me," Ananya noted. "It prevents misunderstandings and conflicts."

Be an active listener

"When we hear something, we usually listen passively, expecting our brains to pick up on the main points and remember them later. However, active listening is an important skill for effective communication. It takes practice to become a better listener, however, it improves our ability to connect with others and retain information."

Communicate effectively

"Communication is essential in our lives, whether at work or in our relationships. This could be the linchpin between failure and success. Due to misunderstandings and issues with delegation, poor communication can cause significant damage."

"Culture, bonding, and socialization of interpersonal relationships all influence relationship dynamics and norms. They are critical for both human development and survival. As a result, people form their first interpersonal relationships as children. However, Vaibhav, it may take a lifetime to better your interpersonal relationships," said Sivaranjan vigilantly.

"I got the point, Uncle," affirmed Vaibhav.

"Me too, Uncle," added Ananya.

How do Interpersonal Relationships Help Boost Teamwork and Success?

"Numerous studies have found that people who have strong relationships with their friends, family, and community members are happier, have fewer health problems, and live longer lives. It has been proven that maintaining interpersonal relationships is critical to our overall health," Sivaranjan explained.

"Wow, I had no idea that relationships could have such a significant impact on our health," Vaibhav responded, amazed.

"Absolutely," Sivaranjan nodded. "Relationships keep us in touch. They assist us in navigating our world, confronting challenges, celebrating victories, and overcoming stressful situations. Good relationships are one of our greatest blessings, even though they require effort. When we invest in interpersonal relationships, we generate feelings of openness, generosity, and goodwill."

Amps Up Your Teamwork Game

"According to research," Sivaranjan continued, "'When members of a team collaborate and share the workload, they feel a greater sense of accomplishment when they complete a task and reach a goal that they would not have been able to achieve if they worked alone. This, when combined with a sense of belonging, appreciation, and recognition, has the potential to significantly improve employee self-esteem and morale.'"

"That makes a lot of sense," Vaibhav said thoughtfully. "I remember feeling proud and connected with my team whenever we successfully completed a project together."

Establishes Stronger Working Relations

"Uncle, I remember a time when my project team in college faced a major hurdle," Ananya said, reflecting on her past experience. "We were working on a group project, and the deadline was approaching fast. One of our team members was going through a tough time personally and wasn't able to contribute much. Initially, some of us were frustrated, thinking he wasn't interested."

"What did you do then?" asked Sivaranjan, curious.

"We decided to talk to him openly. When we found out about his situation, we all agreed to redistribute the work and support him in any way we could. This not only helped us finish the project on time but also strengthened our bond as a team," Vaibhav shared with a smile.

"Exactly, Vaibhav," Sivaranjan nodded approvingly. "You will develop a harmonious relationship with those around you if you respect and understand their concerns. For the team to succeed, asking for help from one another will become routine. The same is true when dealing with your boss and clients. Mutual respect, understanding, open communication, and active listening should all be present. There is a dire need for proper interpersonal skills to handle conversations without a hitch. When this occurs, you will have a better working relationship with your co-workers, employers, customers, and clients."

Builds a Positive Environment at Work

"Everyone thrives in an environment where they feel comfortable and appreciated for their efforts. They will produce positive work results if they are inspired as a result of what they see and hear. These may reflect the calibre of the work they will do," said Sivaranjan.

"Camaraderie and better management will be achieved with improved interpersonal skills," he continued. "They will be more motivated to perform better if their feedback and sentiments are properly heard."

"Improving interpersonal skills is vital for every professional. These skills are essential for achieving greater success whether you work in a company-based office or remotely. They walk with you in every walk of your life," uttered Sivaranjan with wide eyes.

"It is such a simple thing, yet so powerful. My ability to communicate, empathize, work efficiently in a team, and know the people around me better can take me to places. From now on, I will work on my interpersonal skills and bring synergy to the team," said Vaibhav with zeal.

"That's the kind of energy I expect from you, Vaibhav," smiled Sivaranjan.

"Ananya, what about you? Any thoughts?" Sivaranjan asked.

"I've realized how crucial these skills are," Ananya said. "Especially the ability to empathize and communicate effectively. They not only help in achieving professional success but also in creating a positive work environment. I'm excited to apply what I've learned here in my career."

"Interpersonal skills are the backbone of a successful professional life. They are as crucial as your technical skills, if not more. In the corporate world, you will often find that the way you interact with people will determine the opportunities you get, the support you receive, and the overall satisfaction you derive from your work," said Sivaranjan.

"Thank you, uncle. I understand now how vital it is to nurture these relationships. I will make sure to practice and improve my interpersonal skills," Vaibhav said earnestly.

"Good, Vaibhav. Remember, it's a continuous journey. Always be open to learning and growing. You have the potential to achieve great things," said Sivaranjan, encouragingly.

"I'll do the same, uncle," Ananya added. "This has been a real eye-opener for me. I'll focus on building strong interpersonal relationships from the start."

Sivaranjan smiled at both of them. "I'm glad to hear that. Remember, strong interpersonal relationships are the foundation of a successful and fulfilling career. Keep working on them, and you'll see the positive impact on both your professional and personal lives."

Awareness
Reflection
Action

Chapter 13

Understanding Unconscious Bias

Sivaranjan had always believed in the power of diverse perspectives, so he invited his colleague, Neha Singh, to share her insights on a critical topic - unconscious bias in the workplace.

One afternoon, as Vaibhav and Ananya settled in for their usual discussion with Sivaranjan, he began with a tone of anticipation. "Vaibhav, Ananya, today we have something special planned. I've invited a colleague of mine to walk us through a very critical topic that affects every workplace - unconscious bias."

Vaibhav and Ananya exchanged curious glances. "Who is it, Uncle?" Vaibhav asked.

Sivaranjan smiled. "Her name is Neha Singh. She's an expert in organizational behavior and a staunch advocate for equality. Her insights on unconscious bias are invaluable, and it would be beneficial for us to learn from her experiences.

At that moment, Neha entered the room, greeted warmly by Sivaranjan. "Neha, thank you for joining us today. We're eager to learn from your experiences and insights on unconscious bias in the workplace."

Neha smiled and nodded. "Thank you, Sivaranjan. It's a pleasure to be here. Unconscious bias is a topic close to my heart, and I'm glad to have the opportunity to discuss it with you and your mentees."

Sivaranjan turned to Vaibhav and Ananya. "Vaibhav, Ananya, this is Neha. Neha, meet Vaibhav and Ananya, two bright and inquisitive minds eager to learn about the corporate world."

Vaibhav and Ananya greeted Neha enthusiastically. "It's an honor to meet you, Ms. Singh," Ananya said, her eyes reflecting genuine curiosity.

"Likewise," Neha replied warmly. And please call me Neha. "I'm looking forward to indulging in conversations with you both."

Once everyone was settled, Neha asked Sivaranjan if they could begin with the day's learnings.

Sivaranjan gave a nod.

Neha began by posing a thought-provoking question. "Can anyone tell me how many bits of information our brains process every second?"

Ananya and Vaibhav exchanged puzzled looks before Ananya ventured, "I have no idea, maybe a few thousand?"

Neha smiled. *"Our brains process over 11 million bits of information every second. But we can only consciously handle about 40 bits. So, how do we manage the rest?"*

Vaibhav looked intrigued. "We must filter out a lot, right?"

"Exactly," Neha nodded. "We ignore some information, and simplify or generalize other data based on past experiences. This quick, automatic processing helps us make fast decisions, which are crucial for survival, but it also leads to unconscious biases."

She paused, allowing her words to sink in. Vaibhav and Ananya listened intently.

Neha continued, "These biases help us make quick decisions but can also cause unfair treatment of others without us even realizing it. For example, they can creep into job descriptions or interview questions, making certain roles seem more suited for men or women. They influence who gets to speak in meetings, who is heard the most, and even where people sit."

"Wow, I never realized how much our brains filter out," Ananya said, astonished. "It's amazing how these unconscious processes can shape our interactions and decisions."

"Exactly," Neha agreed. ***"Bias can influence every decision and interaction.*** For instance, if a woman is assertive, she might be seen as aggressive, while a man acting the same way might be seen as confident. Managers might overlook mistakes made by employees they like and focus more on the mistakes of those they don't know well. These small, unnoticed biases can add up and create a workplace that feels unfair."

Vaibhav nodded. "It's surprising how these little things can have such a big impact."

Neha smiled. "Yes, and that's why it's important to become aware of and address these biases to create a fair and inclusive workplace."

What is Unconscious Bias?

Neha began, "Before we delve deeper, let me ask you both a question. How do you think biases affect our daily interactions?"

Vaibhav and Ananya looked thoughtful for a moment. Ananya spoke first. "I guess biases make us judge people unfairly, right?"

Neha nodded. "Yes. Now, let's talk about explicit and unconscious biases. Explicit biases are those we openly express. For example, someone might argue that mothers of young children shouldn't hold management positions. But unconscious biases are different because they often lie outside our conscious awareness."

Sivaranjan added, "So, Neha, can you give us an example of unconscious bias in the workplace?"

"Certainly," Neha replied. "Imagine a manager who assigns a tech-heavy task to a young employee instead of an older one. The unspoken assumption here is that younger employees are better tech-savvy. That's unconscious bias at work. It can also occur when team leaders assign less challenging tasks to women, assuming they may not be as capable in technical or leadership roles as their male counterparts."

Vaibhav looked surprised. "I see how that can happen so easily without even realizing it."

"Exactly," Neha continued. "The insidious nature of bias lies in its unconscious aspect. Often, our implicit biases contradict the values we aspire to uphold. And when people aren't even aware that they're doing something, it can be difficult to correct."

Neha paused, giving Ananya and Vaibhav a moment to reflect on the examples she provided. Seeing they were engaged, she continued, "This brings us to another important point. Identifying and understanding our biases is just the beginning. Addressing the challenges and misconceptions around unconscious bias is equally critical."

Challenges and Misconceptions

Ananya raised a point. "What are some common challenges or misconceptions about unconscious bias?"

"One common challenge is resistance to acknowledging bias," Neha said. "Some people may feel defensive or uncomfortable when confronted with their biases. It's important to approach these conversations with empathy and a focus on growth rather than blame.

Another misconception is that bias training alone can solve the problem. While training is important, it must be part of a broader, ongoing effort that includes continuous learning, and a commitment to inclusion at all levels of the organization."

Vaibhav asked, "How can we encourage a culture where people feel comfortable addressing and discussing bias?"

"Creating a safe and supportive environment is crucial," Neha replied. "Encourage open dialogue and ensure that people feel heard and respected. Provide platforms for employees to share their experiences and suggestions. It's also important to have clear policies and procedures in place for reporting and addressing bias and discrimination."

Sivaranjan interjected, "So, Neha, how do we start identifying these unconscious biases in ourselves?"

Neha smiled. "It starts with self-awareness. We need to be mindful of our automatic reactions and question our assumptions. Reflecting on our decisions and seeking feedback from others can also help. It's about creating a habit of introspection and continuous learning."

Identifying Unconscious Bias

Neha said, ***"The first step toward overcoming your unconscious biases is to identify them.*** Reflect on your biases and be proactive in identifying the negative stereotypes you have about others."

Sivaranjan added, "There are several tactics to reduce unconscious biases, summarized by the acronym ***IMPLICIT.*** Neha, could you walk us through these tactics?"

"Of course," Neha replied. "IMPLICIT stands for Introspection, Mindfulness, Perspective-Taking, Learning to Slow Down, Individualization, Checking Your Messaging, Institutionalizing Fairness, and Taking Two. Let's break these down."

Vaibhav leaned forward, eager to learn. "What does Introspection involve?"

Neha explained, "Introspection means setting aside time to understand your biases by taking a personal inventory of them. This can be done by taking tests to identify the biases you may have. Once you're aware of them, you can work on them."

Ananya chimed in, "Now comes Mindfulness?"

"Mindfulness is about being aware that you're more likely to give in to your biases when you're under pressure or need to make quick decisions," Neha answered. "If you're feeling stressed, pause for a minute, collect yourself, and take a few deep breaths."

Vaibhav nodded thoughtfully. "I guess Perspective-Taking is imagining what it would feel like to be stereotyped?"

"Exactly," Neha affirmed. "It helps to put yourself in others' shoes. Think about how it would feel if someone stereotyped you based on your age, gender, or any other characteristic."

Sivaranjan added, "Learning to Slow Down sounds straightforward. Is it about avoiding quick judgments?"

"Yes," Neha replied. "Before jumping to conclusions about others, remind yourself of positive examples of people from their age group, class, ethnicity, or sexual orientation. This can include friends, colleagues, or public figures."

Ananya asked, "What about Individualization?"

Neha responded, "Individualization means recognizing that everyone has unique characteristics.

Focus on the things you have in common with others rather than the stereotypes associated with their group."

Vaibhav looked curious. "How do we check our Messaging?"

"Instead of saying you don't see color, class, or sexual orientation, use statements that embrace inclusivity," Neha said. "For example, Apple Inc.'s inclusion statement emphasizes being different together: 'At Apple, we're not all the same, and that's our greatest strength.'"

Sivaranjan nodded. "Institutionalizing fairness seems important in the workplace. How can we support diversity effectively?"

Neha explained, "Embrace and support diversity by using tools like the Equity and Empowerment Lens, which helps organizations improve planning and resource allocation to foster more equitable policies."

Ananya looked curious. "Neha, can you explain more about the Equity and Empowerment Lens?"

Neha nodded. "The Equity and Empowerment Lens is a tool designed to help organizations improve their planning and resource allocation to foster more equitable policies. It ensures that diverse perspectives are considered in decision-making processes, promoting fairness and inclusion."

"And finally, Take Two?" Vaibhav inquired.

"Overcoming unconscious biases takes time," Neha concluded. "Understand that this is a lifelong process. ***Deprogramming your biases requires constant mindfulness and work. It's about being patient and persistent.***"

Vaibhav and Ananya exchanged thoughtful glances. "This is a lot to take in, however, it makes so much sense," Vaibhav said.

Ananya added, "I never realized how much unconscious biases could affect our daily interactions and decisions."

Sivaranjan smiled. "That's why it's crucial to be aware of them and work on overcoming them."

The Impact of Overcoming Unconscious Bias

Ananya asked, "What impact can overcoming unconscious bias have on an organization?"

"The impact can be profound," Neha said. "Organizations that actively work to overcome unconscious bias often see numerous benefits, including:

1. **Increased Diversity:** A more diverse workforce brings a wider range of perspectives, ideas, and experiences, which can drive innovation and creativity.

2. **Improved Employee Engagement:** When employees feel valued and included, they are more likely to be engaged and motivated, leading to higher productivity and job satisfaction.

3. **Better Decision-Making:** Diverse teams can make better decisions as they consider a wider range of perspectives and avoid groupthink.

4. **Enhanced Reputation:** Organizations that are known for their commitment to diversity and inclusion can attract top talent and build a positive reputation in the marketplace.

5. **Greater Financial Performance:** Studies have shown that organizations with diverse and inclusive cultures often outperform their peers financially.

6. **Stronger Team Dynamics:** Inclusive environments foster collaboration, trust, and respect among team members, leading to stronger team dynamics and better overall performance."

Sivaranjan smiled as Neha concluded her insights. "Thank you, Neha. Your insights have been incredibly valuable. It's clear that addressing unconscious bias requires a commitment to continuous learning and growth, both at the individual and organizational levels."

Neha nodded. "Thank you, Sivaranjan. It's been a pleasure sharing my thoughts with you all. Remember, identifying and addressing unconscious bias is an ongoing journey. ***By staying aware, being open to feedback, and fostering an inclusive culture, we can create a more equitable workplace.***"

Ananya looked inspired. "I'm grateful for this discussion. It has somehow shifted my perspective to things I hadn't considered before."

Vaibhav added, "Absolutely. I now understand how important it is to question our assumptions and be proactive in promoting fairness."

Sivaranjan concluded, "Let's take what we've learned today and apply it in our daily interactions. By doing so, we can make a significant difference in our professional and personal lives. Thank you again, Neha, for your valuable insights and for helping us understand the importance of addressing unconscious bias."

Unity
Equity
Belonging

Chapter 14

Diversity and Inclusion

Sivaranjan gathered Ananya and Vaibhav for another insightful session. "Today also we have Neha joining us to discuss a topic that is the need of the hour," he began, keeping the session's theme a surprise. Both Ananya and Vaibhav looked intrigued as they waited to find out what the discussion would be about.

Soon after, Neha Singh entered the room. Greetings were exchanged, and everyone settled down for yet another topic to unearth.

"Thank you for joining us again, Neha," Sivaranjan said warmly. "We found the last session immersive and insightful on unconscious bias and thought it would be great to hear your thoughts on another crucial topic."

"Thank you for inviting me once again," Neha replied.

Vaibhav leaned forward, curiosity evident on his face. "So, what's today's topic?"

Sivaranjan smiled. "Today, we'll be delving into diversity and inclusion in the workplace."

Ananya's eyes lit up. "That's fantastic."

Neha nodded, "According to Deloitte, diverse companies enjoy 2.3 times higher cash flow per employee. Gartner also found that inclusive teams improve team performance by up to 30 percent in high-diversity environments. However, only 40 percent of employees agree that their manager fosters an inclusive environment."

Vaibhav looked intrigued. "Those are impressive numbers. It's surprising despite the clear benefits, so many managers still fail to create an inclusive environment."

Ananya added, "I agree. It shows there's a significant gap between the potential of diversity and inclusion and what's actually being implemented."

Sivaranjan nodded and turned to Neha. "Neha, we'd love to hear your thoughts on this. Why is there such a gap, and how can we address it?"

Neha said, "We will come to that, first, let us understand what does diversity and inclusion mean."

"Okay," Vaibhav and Ananya said in unison.

Diversity and Inclusion

Neha began, "Simply put, it's an organization's effort, policies, and practices that ensure different groups or individuals from various backgrounds are culturally and socially accepted and integrated into the workplace. *A truly diverse and inclusive organization reflects the society in which it operates.*"

Ananya leaned in, curious. "Can you give us more details about what diversity means in the workplace?"

"Of course," Neha replied. "Diversity refers to the differences in political beliefs, race, culture, sexual orientation, religion, class, and gender identity. In the workplace, this means your staff consists of individuals who bring new perspectives and backgrounds to the table."

Sivaranjan added, "And what about inclusion?"

"Inclusion," Neha explained, "means that everyone in this diverse mix feels involved, valued, respected, treated fairly, and embedded in your culture. *It's about empowering all employees and recognizing their unique talents.*"

Vaibhav nodded thoughtfully. "So, both diversity and inclusion are crucial. What happens if one is missing?"

Neha smiled. "Good question, Vaibhav. Both aspects are important. Diversity without inclusion can result in a toxic culture, while inclusion without diversity can make a company stagnant and uncreative. Many companies are starting to focus more on diversity, but they often neglect the inclusion piece of the puzzle. Without a concerted effort towards both, your workforce will feel out of place and unsupported."

Ananya looked concerned. "It sounds challenging. How do companies ensure they are focusing on both?"

"It's not easy, but it's essential," Neha said. "Creating policies that promote diversity, providing training on inclusion, and fostering an environment where all employees feel they belong are key steps. It's about making sure that every voice is heard and valued."

Sivaranjan summarized, "So, the goal is to build a workplace where everyone feels accepted and valued, reflecting the diverse society we live in."

"Exactly," Neha agreed. "When we focus on both diversity and inclusion, we create a vibrant, innovative, and supportive workplace."

Sivaranjan, wanting to ensure they addressed the question he posed earlier, reminded Neha, "You mentioned earlier the gap between having a diverse team and fostering an inclusive environment. Why do you think this gap exists, and how can we effectively bridge it?"

The Importance of Diversity and Inclusion

Neha began, "Diversity and inclusion are essential for several reasons.

- Firstly, as Sivaranjan mentioned, they lead to better financial performance. Diverse companies are more innovative and have better decision-making capabilities.

- Secondly, inclusion enhances team performance. When team members feel valued and included, they are more engaged and productive.

- Finally, fostering diversity and inclusion improves employee satisfaction and retention. When employees feel a sense of belonging, they are more likely to stay with the company and contribute to its success."

Vaibhav commented, "It seems like a win-win situation. So why do so many companies struggle with this?"

Implementing Diversity and Inclusion

Neha continued, "Implementing diversity and inclusion requires a multifaceted approach. The first step is to create a comprehensive DEIB policy. This policy should outline the company's commitment to diversity, equity, inclusion, and belonging (DEIB) and provide a clear framework for action. It should include specific goals, such as increasing the representation of women in leadership roles, and actionable strategies for achieving these goals."

Ananya jumped in with a follow-up question, "Neha, you mentioned earlier about specific goals like increasing the representation of women in leadership roles. Are there not enough women leaders?"

Neha nodded thoughtfully. "That's a great question, Ananya. Unfortunately, women are still significantly underrepresented in leadership roles. For instance, an analysis of more than 1,100 companies shows that women hold about one-quarter (25.1%) of senior management or leadership roles. That figure is up slightly from 24.0% in 2022 and 23.0% in 2021. This disparity highlights the need for companies to set and achieve specific goals to bridge this gap.

"To increase the representation of women in leadership roles, companies can start by analyzing their current workforce data to identify areas where representation is lacking. From there, they can set measurable objectives, such as increasing the number of women in leadership roles by a certain percentage within a given timeframe.

"To achieve these goals, companies need to implement targeted recruitment strategies, provide mentorship and leadership development programs for underrepresented groups, and ensure there are clear pathways for career advancement. It's also important to hold leadership accountable for progress and to create a culture where diversity and inclusion are actively promoted and valued."

Vaibhav added, "I see. What else can companies do to promote diversity and inclusion?"

Neha continued, "Ensuring that recruitment and hiring practices are fair and unbiased is another critical step. This can be achieved by using diverse interview panels, implementing blind recruitment techniques, and setting diversity targets. Moreover, creating a supportive environment where employees feel safe to share their experiences and concerns is essential. This can be facilitated through open communication channels and regular feedback sessions."

Addressing Challenges and Overcoming Resistance

Sivaranjan asked, "What are some common challenges companies face when implementing DEIB initiatives?"

Neha acknowledged, "There are several challenges. One common challenge is resistance to change. Some employees may feel uncomfortable with new policies and initiatives or may not understand the importance of DEIB. It's important to address these concerns through clear communication and education. Another challenge is the misconception that DEIB training alone can solve the problem. While training is important, it must be part of a broader, ongoing effort that includes policy changes, continuous learning, and a commitment to inclusion at all levels of the organization."

Ananya added, "How can companies overcome this resistance?"

Neha replied, "Creating a culture of inclusion starts from the top. Leadership must demonstrate a genuine commitment to DEIB and lead by example. This means actively participating in DEIB initiatives, holding themselves accountable, and encouraging open dialogue. Additionally, providing ongoing support and resources for employees can help ease the transition and foster a more inclusive environment."

Fostering an Inclusive Culture

Vaibhav asked, "What does an inclusive culture look like?"

Neha explained, "An inclusive culture is one where all employees feel valued, respected, and heard. It's a culture where diversity is celebrated, and everyone has the opportunity to contribute and succeed. This can be achieved by promoting open communication, encouraging collaboration, and recognizing and rewarding diverse contributions. It's also important to create a safe space where employees can share their experiences and concerns without fear of judgment or retaliation."

Ananya remarked, "It sounds like fostering an inclusive culture requires ongoing effort and commitment."

Neha nodded. "Absolutely. DEIB are not one-time initiatives but continuous processes. It's about creating a mindset and culture that values diversity and actively works to include everyone. This requires ongoing education, reflection, and action."

The Role of Female Employees in Diversity and Inclusion

Ananya asked, "How can female employees play a role in promoting diversity and inclusion?"

Neha responded, "Female employees can be powerful advocates for DEIB. By sharing their experiences and perspectives, they can help raise awareness about the unique challenges women face in the workplace. They can also serve as mentors and role models for other women, providing support and guidance. Additionally, women can actively participate in DEIB initiatives, such as ERGs, training programs, and policy development."

Sivaranjan added, "What can organizations do to support female employees in these roles?"

Neha emphasized, "Organizations can support female employees by providing opportunities for leadership and professional development. This includes offering mentorship programs, leadership training, and career advancement opportunities. It's also important to create a supportive and inclusive environment where women feel empowered to speak up and contribute. Recognizing and rewarding the contributions of female employees is another way to show support and encouragement."

Sivaranjan smiled as Neha concluded her insights. "Thank you, Neha, once again. It's clear that addressing diversity and inclusion requires a commitment to continuous learning and growth, both at the individual and organizational levels."

Neha nodded. *"Remember, diversity and inclusion are not just about policies and initiatives; they are about creating a culture where everyone feels valued and included. By working together, we can create a more equitable and inclusive workplace for all."*

Vaibhav and Ananya expressed their gratitude. Vaibhav said, "Thank you, Neha. This discussion has made the importance of diversity and inclusion clear and how we can all play a role in promoting them."

Ananya added, "I appreciate your insights, Neha. I feel more empowered to advocate for diversity and inclusion in my own career, like you."

Neha smiled warmly. "I'm glad to hear that. Remember, each of us has the power to make a difference. Let's continue to learn, grow, and support each other on this journey towards a more inclusive workplace."

Engage
Interpret
Respond
Constructively

Chapter 15

Workplace Conflict - How to Manage it?

"Professionalism is a powerful trait and allows you to live up to the role to the best of your ability. It is not the job you do; it's how you do the job. It allows you to inspire and encourage others. It is something every individual aspires to inculcate in their lives from day one of their professional journeys. Job jitters are normal, interview fright is normal, and seeking help in that time frame is normal," said Sivaranjan addressing both Ananya and Vaibhav.

Sivaranjan contemplated if he could have done things differently. "I appreciate, Vaibhav and Ananya, that you are learning all this. You know, our journey is teaching all of us so much about our desired destination. When I set out on my path, there was no one to guide me. I had to learn through trial and error. But now, being able to guide both of you feels incredibly satisfying. I'm creating a trail for you to tread on in the corporate world, hoping it will be smoother than mine," said Sivaranjan.

Vaibhav and Ananya exchanged glances, feeling the weight of his words.

"We're grateful for your guidance, Uncle," Vaibhav said sincerely. "Your experiences and insights are invaluable to us. It's like having a map for our journey."

"Absolutely," Ananya agreed. "It makes a huge difference knowing we have someone to turn to for advice and support. It gives us confidence to face challenges and to aim higher."

Sivaranjan smiled, feeling a deep sense of fulfilment.

"Remember to be like a tree, for 'a tree that bears the most fruits always bends more towards the ground.' If you want to be great, be humble and show a lot of respect towards your seniors, appreciate your experience and learn from it," said Sivaranjan with a pause.

"Beautiful learning yet again," Vaibhav smiled.

"When we talk about the corporate world, the scenario is not always happy-chirpy, peaceful, or friendly. There exists competition, and to stay ahead of the competition you have to pitch good ideas and innovative solutions, and it requires human interaction which can result in arguments, debates, and conflicts," said Sivaranjan in a tense voice.

"Let's understand what conflicts are and how they take place," said Sivaranjan.

What are Workplace Conflicts?

"When employees with different backgrounds and priorities work together in any organization, conflict arises. Conflict can be expressed in a variety of ways, including bullying, insults, non-cooperation, and anger. Personality clashes and misunderstood communication can all contribute to it, as organizational mismanagement. Workplace conflict can lead to work disruptions, decreased productivity, project failure, absenteeism, turnover, and termination. It can be both a cause and an effect of emotional stress," explained Sivaranjan.

"A study has identified the human behavior that is responsible for conflicts. 'These traits proceed to cause distressing events that impact the safety and well-being of anyone who comes in contact with them. They have an impact on the well-being of co-workers and customers, which affects organizational productivity.'"

"Up until recently, most organizations viewed workplace conflict as entirely negative. However, as it turns out, there is some value in workplace conflict, and it can bring some benefits to a company, such as:

- Employees' creativity has spiked.

- An open and truthful exchange of ideas.

- Employees compete to improve their skills.

- A challenge to the status quo can lead to innovation."

"Everything in life has two facets, and conflicts are no exception. The only thing that needs to be taken care of is to handle or manage the conflict," said Sivaranjan.

"As you know, every individual is unique and has their way of facing, reacting to, or tackling a situation. Let's understand different conflict management styles," said Sivaranjan.

"Yes, uncle, let's set the course," said Ananya.

What are the Conflict Management Styles?

"Vaibhav and Ananya, you must have seen that every individual has a different approach to manage conflicts. However, have you ever thought about why it happens? We all have different conflict management styles that make us react in any situation," explained Sivaranjan.

"In 1974, two researchers, Kenneth W. Thomas, and Ralph H. Kilmann studied employees and their routine workplace conflicts. They were able to observe a pattern of how people resolved the conflict over time; most methods could be distilled down to five core methods. The Thomas Kilmann Conflict Mode Instrument and the Thomas Kilmann Conflict Resolution Model were built on these five options."

"Let's understand them better with a metaphor - a five-year-old boy came home whining. His father/mother/elder asked what happened. He said that his classmate hit him. Now, based on the response they will tell the child, the child will get conditioned to that particular style unknowingly. For example, they told him to hit them back, stay away from them or say sorry, so on and so forth."

"Let us understand styles in detail," said Sivaranjan.

1. Avoiding – Turtle

His father/mother/elder tells him to pick another place to play if something like that happens again. If the same situation arises, the boy chooses to play someplace else. He learns to avoid conflict, like a turtle retreating into its shell, physically and psychologically avoiding the situation rather than facing it."

Ananya nodded thoughtfully. "So, it's like avoiding confrontation to keep the peace, even if it means not addressing the issue directly."

2. Competing - Shark

His father/mother/elder advises him to fight back and beat the other boy the next time. The boy grasps that he needs to dominate the situation to avoid being bullied. This style, like a shark, is all about winning, no matter who the opponent is. Sharks are designed to win at all costs," Sivaranjan explained.

Vaibhav raised an eyebrow. "That sounds aggressive. So, it's about asserting dominance and coming out on top, no matter what?"

"Yes, that's correct," Sivaranjan replied..

3. Accommodating - Teddy

His father/mother/elder tells him to go and make up with the other boy and not to fight with friends. The boy learns to value relationships over conflict, trying to sort things out amicably. This is the teddy style, where you accommodate others to maintain harmony, negotiating and resolving the conflict peacefully," Sivaranjan continued.

Ananya smiled. "Like a teddy bear, focusing on keeping relationships intact and avoiding fights."

Note: The above three styles are the ancestral styles that we learn from our elders, parents, teachers, or guardians. The next two are the styles that we learn through our experiences, setbacks, and achievements.

4. Compromising - Fox

The fox style involves being assertive and cooperative but with a readiness to give up something to reach a middle ground. It's like bargaining, where both parties give and take to arrive at a mutually acceptable solution," Sivaranjan elaborated.

Vaibhav interjected, "So, a compromise might leave everyone a bit unsatisfied, but it's often better than a stalemate or conflict, right?"

"Exactly," Sivaranjan confirmed. "A good compromise leaves nobody completely satisfied but is often the best alternative."

5. Collaborating - Owl

Finally, the owl style implies being high on both the task and the relationship. Owls see conflict as a problem to solve together. They believe there must be a solution and view conflict as an opportunity to strengthen relationships and achieve their objectives," Sivaranjan concluded.

Ananya reflected, "So, collaborating means addressing the problem directly but also ensuring that the relationship is strengthened in the process."

"Yes," said Sivaranjan. "Owls are wise. They look for solutions that satisfy all parties and see conflicts as opportunities for growth and understanding."

Vaibhav added, "It seems like collaborating is the ideal approach, however, it probably requires more effort and communication than the other styles."

"Indeed," Sivaranjan agreed. "But it's often the most rewarding and effective in the long run."

"These are the five conflict management styles, and if we have to decide upon which one is right or wrong. Well, all of them are right, and all of them are wrong. However, it is better to be a teddy than a turtle because if you remain a turtle, it will be challenging for people to put their faith and trust in you. People will assume that you will go somewhere else to avoid the situation. It is better to be a shark as they are visible in the system or a teddy as relationship -oriented individuals can take you a long way. However, your ultimate motive should be to be an owl. You should put in a conscious effort to become an owl in the system," Sivaranjan elaborated.

"I hope you both have understood the conflict management styles. Now, let's learn to deal with the conflicts at the workplace," said Sivaranjan.

"Yes, uncle, you explained the concepts so distinguishingly that they are ingrained in my memory," said Vaibhav and Ananya nodded in agreement.

How to Handle Conflict at the Workplace?

"Conflicts in organizations are as real as we humans. They can happen at any level of the hierarchy. If you ever find yourself amidst a conflict, and you want to get to its roots, start thinking of what could have gone

wrong 'on your part.' People are good with playing the blame game; you have to think beyond that and be a bigger person by scrutinizing the matter at hand well," explained Sivaranjan.

"You need to see if you have to make any changes on your end. If you played a part (even a smaller part) in the conflict, you have to stand up to it and accept it with humility. You have to find the learning in disguise, and it requires a great length of emotional maturity to handle such situations."

"Uncle, I remember a time when I had a disagreement with a teammate during a group project. Initially, I blamed him for the issue, but after reflecting on my actions, I realized I had also contributed to the conflict by not communicating clearly and effectively," said Ananya.

"That's a valuable realization, Ananya," replied Sivaranjan. "Taking responsibility for your part in a conflict is the first step towards resolution. It shows maturity and a willingness to improve the situation."

"Absolutely, uncle. But how should we approach the other person once we've realized our part in the conflict?" asked Vaibhav.

"Good question, Vaibhav. Here are some steps you can follow to handle conflict at the workplace effectively," said Sivaranjan.

Look at the 'importance' factor

"If an issue is important enough to spark a conflict, it must be important enough to resolve. People will do whatever it takes to open lines of communication and close positional and/or philosophical gaps if the issue, circumstance, or situation is important enough and there is enough at stake," advised Sivaranjan.

"I agree, Uncle," said Ananya. "When something matters to everyone involved, there's a natural drive to find common ground or at least understand each other's perspectives better."

Face the conflict

"While you can't always avoid conflicts, the key to conflict resolution is to face them whenever possible. By actively seeking out potential areas of conflict and intervening in a just and decisive manner, you can likely prevent certain conflicts from arising. If a conflict does arise, dealing with it quickly will likely reduce its severity. Time spent identifying and comprehending natural tensions will aid in the avoidance of unnecessary conflict. Separate the person from the problem; sometimes we do not separate them and get emotionally charged," Sivaranjan continued.

"I remember a time in our project group," Vaibhav shared. "There was tension brewing, and I realized later we could have addressed it earlier. It's true that letting conflicts linger only makes them worse."

Understand 'what's in it for you'

"Before weighing in, it is critical to understand the motivations of others. To avoid conflict, assist those around you in achieving their goals. If you approach conflict from the standpoint of taking the action that will best help others achieve their goals, you will find that few obstacles will stand in your way of resolving conflict," explained Sivaranjan.

"That's insightful," nodded Ananya. "When we focus on how resolving conflicts can benefit everyone involved, it shifts the approach from adversarial to collaborative."

Look at the conflict as an opportunity

"There is amazing potential for teaching or learning opportunities in every conflict. It contains the inherent potential for development and growth in disagreements. When divergent perspectives are handled correctly, they can stimulate learning and innovation in ample ways that our minds cannot even imagine. Smart leaders look at the positive side of every situation," said Sivaranjan.

"You both are still in the budding stages of professionalism and should learn from everything you come across in the organization. That's how you evolve, that's how you get into good positions, and that's how you teach your subordinates about facing challenging situations. If the underlying desire is strong enough, turning the other cheek, compromising, forgiveness, compassion, empathy, finding common ground, being an active listener, service above self, and a variety of other approaches will always allow you to be successful in building rapport. When all else fails and it seems impossible to close the positional gaps, resolve the issue by doing the right thing rather than playing favorites," said Sivaranjan.

"I will bear these points in mind and keep making my way to being successful. I have understood my role in any conflict. I will always be vigilant and keep these learnings in mind to handle any challenging situation," said Vaibhav.

Ananya reflected, "It's reassuring to know that conflicts aren't just obstacles but opportunities for growth. Understanding each other's perspectives and focusing on collective goals can truly transform how conflicts are resolved in any organization."

"If you stay true and committed to your work, you will stay out of the hay," said Sivaranjan.

Stop Dwelling
Start Doing
Find Solution

Chapter 16

Problem-solving and Decision-making

Before heading for our next topic, let me ask you both a question, said Sivaranjan.

Sivaranjan began, "imagine a few kids were playing near the railway tracks. One was playing on the abandoned track while the others were playing on the live tracks. A passenger train is approaching the kids, and they are busy playing, unaware of the danger. You find yourself near the lever that can change the track of the train. What would you do? Would you change the course to the abandoned track and save most of the kids while sacrificing the one playing alone? Or would you rather let the train take its original course?"

Vaibhav thought for a moment and then responded, "I think I would change the track to save the majority of the kids, even if it meant sacrificing the one."

Sivaranjan nodded thoughtfully. "Most people would probably choose to change the train's route and sacrifice only one child. But did you consider that the child who chose to play on the abandoned track had made the correct decision to play in a safe location? Nonetheless, he had to be sacrificed because his friends chose to play on working and utterly dangerous tracks."

Ananya frowned, considering the dilemma. "It does seem unfair that the child who made the right choice should suffer because of the others."

"Exactly," Sivaranjan agreed. "This type of quandary occurs all the time. The scenario teaches us another lesson: while we make decisions in our lives, it is our moral responsibility to teach others about the repercussions of making choices. If we do not do this, we may end up like the boy in this scenario. All of them would be safe and sound if the kid chose to ask his friends to play on the abandoned track."

Sivaranjan paused, then added, "But let's add another perspective. What if, by changing the route of the train to the abandoned track, there is a chance the train could overturn because it's not designed to handle the weight of a train? This could risk the lives of the passengers on board. Now, what would you do?"

Vaibhav's eyes widened as he pondered the new information. "That's even more complicated. If the train overturns, it could cause even more harm."

"Indeed," Sivaranjan said. ***Sometimes, decisions are not just about the immediate consequences but also about the potential risks and broader impacts.*** In such scenarios, it's essential to weigh all factors carefully before making a decision. While we are all aware that life is full of difficult decisions that must be made, we may fail to recognize that hasty decisions are not always the best ones. Keep in mind that what is right is not always popular, and what is popular is not always right."

Vaibhav nodded slowly, absorbing the lesson. "I understand, uncle. It's about more than just the immediate choice—it's about considering all possible outcomes and ensuring everyone understands the consequences of their actions."

"Exactly," Sivaranjan smiled. "In the corporate world, you will face many such dilemmas. Always strive to make informed decisions and guide others to do the same."

Ananya interjected, "Uncle Sivaranjan, I remember a similar discussion we had during our Ethics class in college. We debated scenarios like these where ethical decisions weren't straightforward. It taught us the importance of critical thinking and considering all perspectives before making a choice."

Sivaranjan nodded approvingly. "That's right, Ananya. College is a great place to start honing your problem-solving and decision-making skills. What were some challenging decisions you faced during group projects or debates?"

Ananya reflected, "We often had to decide on project directions where each member had different ideas. It was challenging to balance everyone's perspectives while ensuring we stayed on track to meet our deadlines."

"That sounds familiar," Vaibhav added. "We faced similar challenges. Sometimes, deciding whether to pursue an innovative but risky idea or a safer, more traditional approach was a dilemma."

"Yes," Sivaranjan nodded. "These experiences in college prepare you for the complexities you'll face in your career. Problem-solving and decision-making skills are crucial in both academic and professional settings."

Sivaranjan said with a smile. "Let's understand problem-solving and decision-making in detail."

What are Problem-solving and Decision-making?

"Every day, we use our creativity to solve problems," Sivaranjan continued. "For example, you may need to change your route due to traffic, troubleshoot an IT problem, or figure out what to make for dinner using the ingredients left in the fridge. Your professional challenges are likely to be more complicated than these examples, but the skills and processes you use to find solutions are largely the same, as they rely on your ability to analyze a situation and decide on a course of action."

"Problem-solving and decision-making are crucial in any job, so it's important to show that you have the resilience and skills to view problems as challenges, make sound choices, and learn and grow from your experiences."

"Uncle," Vaibhav interjected, "in college, we make decisions quickly, especially during group projects. Sometimes it's overwhelming."

"That's a perfect example," Sivaranjan said. "Problem-solving and decision-making are not limited to professional settings. They are skills you will use throughout your life."

What are the Different Steps to Solve a Problem?

"Let's break down the steps to solve a problem," Sivaranjan suggested. "The first step is to define the problem."

Define the Problem

"Most people jump to conclusions while defining a problem, which means they are looking for the solution in the problem itself. *It is said that when a problem is well-defined, it is 80% solved.* This can be done in a variety of ways, including:

- Identifying the gap between the current state and the desired state.

- Asking questions to clarify the problem and its context.

- Breaking down the problem into smaller, more manageable pieces.

- Defining the problem in specific, measurable terms.

Effective problem definition is important because it sets the stage for the rest of the problem-solving process. *A clearly defined problem allows you to focus your efforts and resources on finding a solution that addresses the root cause of the issue.*"

"Uncle, in our group project, we did struggle to define the problem clearly," Ananya admitted.

"That's common, Ananya," Sivaranjan replied. "Using tools like a problem statement and symptom worksheet can help."

Problem Statement and Symptom Worksheet

"A problem statement is a concise description of an issue that needs to be addressed or a condition that needs to be improved upon. It should be specific and state what needs to be resolved, but not suggest any solutions.

A symptom worksheet is a tool used to gather and organize information about a problem or issue. It is typically used to identify the symptoms of a problem, as well as the possible causes and impacts of those symptoms. The purpose of a symptom worksheet is to help you better understand the problem you are trying to solve and to guide your efforts in finding a solution."

"Can you give me an example of a symptom worksheet, uncle?" Vaibhav asked while looking at Ananya to see if she has the same question.

Ananya nodded.

"Sure," Sivaranjan said. "Here's an example:

Symptom: Product defects

Possible causes:

Poor quality raw materials

Incorrect manufacturing processes

Lack of maintenance on equipment

Impacts:

Increased customer complaints

Reduced productivity

Increased production costs

Using a symptom worksheet can help you to clearly define the problem and identify potential causes, which can then be used to generate and evaluate potential solutions," explained Sivaranjan.

Analyzing the Problem

"It is an important step in the problem-solving process," Sivaranjan continued. "It involves breaking down the problem into smaller pieces and understanding it in more depth. Here are some steps you can follow to analyze a problem:

Gather information: Collect all relevant information about the problem, including any constraints or limitations.

Identify the root cause: Determine what is causing the problem. This may require breaking the problem down into smaller pieces and looking at each piece separately.

Consider the impacts: Think about how the problem is affecting you, others, and the broader system.

Look for patterns: Look for any patterns or trends in the data you have collected.

Generate hypotheses: Based on your analysis, come up with possible explanations for the problem.

By thoroughly analyzing the problem, you can better understand its complexity and develop more effective solutions."

"Uncle, we often miss the root cause in our analysis," Vaibhav confessed.

Ananya added, "I've also found that discussing the problem with team members who have different perspectives can uncover insights we might have missed individually."

"Collaboration indeed plays a vital role," Sivaranjan remarked. ***Each team member brings unique experiences and viewpoints that enrich the analysis process.***

Vaibhav considered this. "So, by integrating these methods into our problem-solving approach, we not only identify the root cause more effectively but also develop more robust solutions."

"Exactly," Sivaranjan affirmed. "And these skills will serve you well in your future career endeavors. Problem-solving is not just about finding quick fixes but about understanding the complexities and making informed decisions."

"That's why using tools like ***root-cause analysis*** and the ***Five-Why Analysis*** can be helpful," Sivaranjan suggested.

The Five-Why Analysis

"It identifies the root cause of a problem by repeatedly asking the question 'why.' It involves asking why the problem occurred and then asking why again for each answer until the root cause is identified."

"Can you walk us through an example, Uncle?" Ananya asked.

"Of course," Sivaranjan replied. "Here's an example:

Problem: A machine is producing defective parts.

- **Why did the machine produce defective parts?** Because the machine was not properly maintained.

- **Why was the machine not properly maintained?** Because the maintenance schedule was not followed.

- **Why was the maintenance schedule not followed?** Because the maintenance technician was not trained on how to follow the schedule.

- **Why was the maintenance technician not trained on how to follow the schedule?** Because the training documentation was not updated.

- **Why was the training documentation not updated?** Because the person responsible for updating it was on leave and no one else was trained to do it.

By asking 'why' five times, we were able to identify the root cause of the problem (the outdated training documentation) and can now take steps to address it."

"The Five Whys technique is simple and can be effective in quickly identifying the root cause of a problem," Vaibhav remarked.

"Exactly," Sivaranjan agreed. "How do you know you have found the root cause?" Sivaranjan continued. "There are a few signs that you have found the root cause of a problem:

Root-Cause Analysis

"This is a problem-solving technique used to identify the underlying cause of a problem. It is a systematic approach to finding the cause of a problem, rather than just addressing the symptoms.

The goal is to identify the root cause of a problem so that it can be addressed, rather than just treating the symptoms. By addressing the root cause, you can prevent the problem from occurring again in the future."

The root cause addresses the problem: When you have identified the root cause of a problem, it should directly address the issue you are trying to solve.

The root cause is actionable: The root cause should be something that you can take action on. If you can't do anything to address the root cause, then it's likely not the real root cause.

The root cause is supported by evidence: The root cause should be based on evidence and data, rather than assumptions or guesses.

The root cause makes sense: The root cause should make logical sense and fit with what you know about the problem.

The root cause is confirmed: Once you have identified the root cause, it's important to confirm that it is indeed the root cause. This can be done through testing or further investigation.

If you have found the root cause of a problem, it should address the issue, be actionable, be supported by evidence, make sense, and be confirmed."

"Understanding these aspects of root cause analysis will not only help in problem-solving but also in ensuring that we address issues at their core, leading to more effective and lasting solutions," Ananya and Vaibhav agreed.

Optimal Solution Construction

"This is the process of selecting the best solution to a problem. Here are some steps you can follow to construct an optimal solution:

Generate potential solutions: Come up with as many potential solutions as you can.

Evaluate the potential solutions: Consider the pros and cons of each potential solution.

Select the best solution: Choose the solution that best addresses the problem and meets any constraints or requirements.

Develop a plan: Create a plan to implement the selected solution.

Communicate the plan: Share the plan with relevant stakeholders and get their feedback and buy-in.

Implement the plan: Put the plan into action.

Monitor and adjust: Monitor the implementation of the plan and make any necessary adjustments.

Constructing an optimal solution involves generating and evaluating potential solutions, selecting the best one, and developing a plan to implement it. It is important to communicate the plan and get feedback from stakeholders, and to monitor and adjust the implementation as needed."

"When you reach the finish line on your problem-solving and decision-making process, implement the solution, and make sure to track your solution's progress," Sivaranjan advised. "Did the solution eliminate the problem? If the outcome is not the way you wanted it to be, then you can spiral back to the problem and find another solution."

They both listened intently. "These methods work as a roadmap to solve the problem, and you will also need to understand different problem-solving and decision-making styles to understand other individuals' perspectives towards the problem."

"Effective problem-solving and decision-making require strong analytical and critical thinking skills, as well as the ability to think creatively and consider multiple perspectives," Sivaranjan explained. "It can also be helpful to develop good communication and collaboration skills, as these can help facilitate a more productive and effective problem-solving and decision-making process."

"I understood it well, uncle," Vaibhav said. "Problem-solving and decision-making involve choosing between different options or courses of action. It requires the ability to evaluate the pros and cons of each option and to select the one that is most likely to be effective."

"Indeed, Vaibhav," Sivaranjan said with a smile. **"There will be times when you will find yourself** *surrounded by a dilemma, confusion, and quick thinking. It is then that problem-solving and decision-making skills will drag you out of the situation."*

Ananya nodded in agreement. "I've realized from our discussion today that problem-solving isn't just about finding solutions; it's about approaching challenges with a strategic mindset. It's reassuring to know that these skills are applicable both personally and professionally."

"This conversation has been really enlightening, uncle," Vaibhav said. "I feel more confident about approaching problems in a structured way now."

"That's the goal, Vaibhav," Sivaranjan replied warmly. "Always remember to pause, analyze, and make informed decisions. You'll find that this approach will serve you well in both your personal and professional life."

Ananya said, "I'm grateful for the insights shared today, Uncle Sivaranjan. Understanding the importance of thorough analysis and informed decision-making will definitely shape how I tackle challenges moving forward."

Sivaranjan nodded, pleased. "Absolutely, Ananya. Continuously honing these skills will set you both apart in your careers. Remember, every challenge is an opportunity to grow."

Radiate
Share
Illuminate

Chapter 17

Consistent Positive Mental Attitude

"Let me give you both an example," Sivaranjan began. "We all know about Sachin Tendulkar, a cricket legend, a leading run-scorer, and a century-maker in Test and One Day International cricket. He is the only player thus far to score one hundred international centuries, the first batsman to score a double century in an ODI, and the holder of the record for the greatest number of runs in both ODI and Test cricket."

"Tendulkar retired from cricket in 2013. He became the youngest player in history to score a Test fifty. Tendulkar, who was only 16 at the time, accomplished this feat during the second Test match between India and Pakistan in Faisalabad in 1989. He faced a pace battery led by the buoyant Imran Khan along with Wasim Akram and Waqar Younis," Sivaranjan elaborated.

"Facing such fast bowlers seems terrifying," Vaibhav remarked.

"Indeed, facing such fast bowlers was not for faint-hearted players, and Sachin stood his ground even after getting hit on the nose. He would have stepped back when he got hurt, instead, he thought through his injury and then decided to stick to the crease for the next 30 minutes to get used to the pace. He carried on and emerged with flying colors. Tendulkar and Sanjay Manjrekar stitched a 143-run partnership for the fifth wicket in that match when India was struggling at 101/4," Sivaranjan continued.

"That's true resilience," Ananya said, impressed.

"He played valiantly that day, his upbeat demeanor and positive attitude got him accolades all over the world. Tendulkar etched his name in history as the 'greatest batter of all time,' and he was also anointed the 'Master Blaster,'" Sivaranjan concluded.

"So, it was his attitude towards the situation that made him stand firm that day and he became the country's favorite cricketer in that instant," Vaibhav reflected.

"Absolutely, Vaibhav. ***When a person breathes a positive attitude, he can make anything possible,*** ***Sivaranjan said.***

"Another powerful example of a consistently positive mental attitude is Kapil Dev," Sivaranjan continued.

"Kapil Dev, the Haryana Hurricane, right?" Ananya asked.

"Yes, he is considered one of the greatest all-rounders and one of the greatest fast bowlers in the history of cricket. He is best known for leading the Indian cricket team to their first World Cup victory in 1983. Nobody thought the underdog team would knock the wind out of the West Indies, a nearly unbeatable cricket team of that time," Sivaranjan explained.

"How did they manage that?" Vaibhav asked eagerly.

"The entire tournament was an upheaval for the Indian cricket team as not a soul believed that India would hoist the World Cup Trophy on the Lord's balcony. Right from the beginning, the Indian cricket team was mocked to show the audacity to play for the World Cup. The only person who believed in taking home the trophy was Kapil Dev, who said, 'We are here to win the World Cup, what else are we here for,' when an interviewer asked, 'What are your team's chances in the World Cup?'" Sivaranjan recounted.

"That must have taken a lot of confidence," Vaibhav noted.

"Everyone in the room laughed at his answer, even his team thought he was out of his mind to think like that, to beat two-time World Cup winner - West Indies.

However, Kapil kept saying they would win the World Cup, no matter the dwindling hopes to win," Sivaranjan continued.

"And they did win!" Ananya said, smiling.

"Yes, gradually his team picked up the right attitude and started showing sheer individual brilliance on the field. Finally, India beat the mighty West Indies by 43 runs to script history at Lord's," Sivaranjan concluded.

"A consistent positive mental attitude can do wonders and have a powerful impact on an individual's overall well-being. It leads to increased resilience in the face of challenges, improved mood and self-esteem, and better relationships with others. It leads to better decision-making and problem-solving abilities in challenging situations," Sivaranjan explained.

Neuroscience and Positive Attitude

"Uncle, how does neuroscience back up all this?" Vaibhav asked.

"Neuroscience research suggests that a positive mental attitude can be contagious. When people interact with others who have a positive attitude, it can be infectious and can rub off on them, influencing their mood and outlook. A positive attitude can also create a more supportive and productive environment, leading to better communication and collaboration among team members. Studies have shown that individuals who work in positive environments tend to be more engaged, motivated, and productive," Sivaranjan explained.

"That's truly fascinating," Vaibhav said. "It will be life-long ingrained in my mind."

"I agree, Uncle," Ananya added. "I've noticed that when I'm around positive people, I feel more energized and optimistic. It's like their positivity lifts everyone's spirits."

"Exactly, Ananya," Sivaranjan said, nodding. "A positive mental attitude doesn't just benefit the individual; it can uplift an entire group. When you maintain a positive outlook, you not only improve your own experiences but also contribute to a more positive environment for others."

What is a Consistent Positive Mental Attitude?

"So, let's venture into the realm of consistent positive mental attitude today," Sivaranjan suggested.

"I cannot wait," Vaibhav said eagerly.

"A consistent positive mental attitude (CPMA) means looking at every situation and challenge in life with optimism. This concept was first introduced by author Napoleon Hill in his 1937 self-help book 'Think and Grow Rich.' Throughout the book, he explains how having the right mindset attracts good things and increases your chances of success," Sivaranjan explained.

"I've heard of that book," Ananya said.

"Later, Hill elaborated on the topic by writing a separate book titled 'Success Through a Positive Mental Attitude.' This best-seller teaches readers that their mindset and attitude affect their health, happiness, and success. A positive mindset, according to the positive mental attitude philosophy, is synonymous with hope, optimism, courage, and kindness. It also means resisting negativity and hopelessness, even in difficult circumstances," Sivaranjan continued.

"That sounds like a powerful approach," Vaibhav remarked.

"When times are tough, you can manage your emotions positively and constructively with a positive mental attitude. A positive mental attitude is a choice. It promises that by choosing to see the positive side of life and make the best of any situation, you will create a better reality for yourself," Sivaranjan explained.

Ananya nodded thoughtfully. "I think that makes a lot of sense. I've noticed that when I approach my studies or projects with a positive attitude, I not only feel better, but I also perform better. It's like my mindset can actually change the outcome."

"Absolutely, Ananya," Sivaranjan agreed. "Our thoughts and our words have a powerful influence on our reality. When we believe in positive outcomes, we're more likely to take actions that lead to those outcomes."

Vaibhav added, "I remember during our final exams, Ananya. I was stressed out, but I kept saying I'd do well, and it helped me stay focused and calm. I guess that was an example of CPMA in action."

Ananya smiled. "Yes, it was. I believe that if you expect good things to happen, you're more open to opportunities and solutions."

"That's the essence of CPMA," Sivaranjan said. "It's about training your mind to stay positive, no matter the circumstances. It doesn't mean ignoring problems or challenges, but rather facing them with a hopeful and proactive attitude."

"How can we cultivate a consistent positive mental attitude in our daily lives?" Vaibhav asked.

"Start by being mindful of your thoughts," Sivaranjan advised. "When you catch yourself thinking negatively, try to reframe those thoughts into something positive. Surround yourself with positive influences, whether it's people, books, or activities. And practice gratitude—focus on what you're thankful for, even the small things. Over time, these habits will help you maintain a consistent positive mental attitude."

Ananya added, "I think it's also important to be kind to yourself. Sometimes we can be our own worst critics. Practicing self-compassion can help us stay positive, even when we make mistakes."

"Well said, Ananya," Sivaranjan responded. "Self-compassion is a key component of CPMA. When we're kind to ourselves, we're better equipped to handle setbacks and challenges with a positive outlook."

Vaibhav nodded. "I'm going to start paying more attention to my thoughts and try to stay positive, even when things get tough."

"That's the spirit, Vaibhav," Sivaranjan encouraged. "Remember, a consistent positive mental attitude is a powerful tool that can transform your life. Keep practicing it, and you'll see the benefits in every aspect of your journey."

Hallmarks of Positive Mental Attitude

"Jim Carrey, a major Hollywood star, is a firm believer in the power of a positive mindset. Long before he became a successful superstar, he began to believe that he would get there someday. He wrote himself a check for $10 million, gave himself a timeline of 5 years, and dated it Thanksgiving 1995. Right before Thanksgiving 1995, he found out that he was going to make $10 million on

Dumb and Dumber. And, later he buried the check with his father," Sivaranjan shared.

"It's hard to believe that these techniques helped Carrey become one of the world's biggest stars," Ananya said, amazed.

"When Oprah questioned him, he said that hard work was the real key to success. 'Well, yeah, that's the thing, you can't just visualize and then go get a sandwich,' Carrey said," Sivaranjan recounted with a smile.

"So, it's about visualizing and working hard towards it," Vaibhav noted.

"Exactly, Vaibhav. Here are some hallmarks of a positive mental attitude," Sivaranjan said.

1. Embracing Acceptance over Resistance

"Our instinct is to categorize situations as either favorable or unfavorable. But what if we refrained from this judgment and simply embraced things as they are? This concept is known as radical acceptance. By adopting this mindset, we eliminate the negativity that often arises when things don't go as planned, allowing us to respond more effectively to any circumstance," Sivaranjan explained.

"How do we practice that?" Vaibhav asked.

"Resistance tends to create stagnation, preventing us from fully experiencing the present. However, wheOn we accept our current reality, we shift our focus to constructive actions, asking ourselves, 'Given this situation, what can I do now?'" Sivaranjan continued.

"Things happen in life that are beyond our control, but the way we respond to them makes all the difference in our experience," Ananya reflected.

2. Courage

"Imagination is another name for courage and worry is the misuse of imagination," Sivaranjan said.

"Courage allows you to pursue your goals without fear of failure, rejection, or other irrational fears. Instead of being afraid of failure, courageous people view it as an opportunity to learn. This positive mindset makes it easier to achieve your goals and grow personally and professionally."

"Chetna Gala Sinha, a resident of a rural village community, shares stories of successful initiatives undertaken by the women of her village at a TED event in Vancouver. She describes their struggles and trials, as well as how they persisted in taking control of their lives on their own. 'My courage is my capital,' she says," Sivaranjan shared.

3. Practice Gratitude

"People who are grateful for even the smallest things in life are happier and healthier. They express and feel gratitude for the good things in their lives, such as family, good health, or even a sunny day. Keeping a gratitude journal is a common practice among those with a positive mindset," Sivaranjan explained.

"Oprah started a gratitude journal sixteen years ago and began writing down five things she was grateful for every day. Oprah says that acknowledging the goodness in her life, from fresh flowers to the kindness of a stranger, made her more receptive to it," Sivaranjan continued.

"I can see how that could change someone's outlook on life," Ananya said thoughtfully.

4. Resilience

"It is defined in positive psychology as the ability to recover from stressful and challenging life events. Resilient people deal with difficult situations with ease and do not succumb to negative emotions during difficult times," Sivaranjan explained.

"Gautam Adani, founder, and chairman of the Adani Group, did not have an easy ticket to success. He faced tremendous adversities early in his life. He had to drop out of his graduation and start working as a diamond sorter in Mumbai due to a financial crunch.

However, the young Adani was not deterred by his early setbacks, and he established a diamond trading business, earning his first million by the age of 20. Adani persisted and, in a short period, established one of India's most well-known business houses, an $8 billion professionally managed empire," Sivaranjan recounted.

"That's truly inspiring. Resilience seems to be a key trait for success," Vaibhav noted.

5. Appreciate Small Wins

"It can be an important part of maintaining a positive mental attitude. It can help you focus on your success, rather than dwelling on your failures or shortcomings. It can help to break down large goals into smaller, more manageable steps, making it easier to see progress and feel a sense of accomplishment. Celebrating small wins can also help to boost self-esteem, and make individuals feel good about themselves and their abilities," Sivaranjan explained.

"According to Harvard Business School researcher Teresa Amabile, people who tracked their small achievements every day increased their motivation. The simple practice of tracking your progress allows you to appreciate your small victories, which boosts your confidence and performance," Sivaranjan added.

"That's a good practice. I think I should start tracking my small wins," Vaibhav said.

"Absolutely, Vaibhav," Ananya said. "I've noticed that when I celebrate even the smallest achievements, like completing a chapter of a textbook or hitting a milestone in a project, it keeps me motivated to keep going. It feels rewarding and reminds me that I'm making progress."

"That's a great insight, Ananya," Sivaranjan said. "Celebrating small wins can indeed provide that motivation boost and reinforce the positive mental attitude we're striving for."

Vaibhav nodded. "I'm definitely going to give it a try. It's easy to get bogged down by everything that still needs to be done, but acknowledging what I've already accomplished should help me stay positive."

"A positive mental attitude in life and at work is a powerful skill. It helps you overcome adversity as well as enhances your coping mechanisms," Sivaranjan concluded.

How to Maintain a Consistent Positive Mental Attitude?

"Uncle, I understand the concept well. Could you please tell me the ways to maintain a positive mental attitude?" Vaibhav asked.

"Yes, please, Uncle," added Ananya.

"Yes, we are getting there," Sivaranjan replied. "We can cultivate optimism through the way we think and act. Let me elaborate on it."

Change Your Perspective

"Change your perspective and it can positively influence your life. By simply rephrasing your sentences, you can take it as an opportunity to do something productive. Assume you are accompanying your father to the bank. This may appear to be a chore at first. 'I have to take my father to the bank,' you think to yourself. Instead of 'I have to' say 'I get to,'" Sivaranjan explained.

"In other words, consider this moment as a chance to spend some time with your father in your hectic schedule. It will make a difference," Vaibhav completed the thought.

"Always smile and treat people with kindness, and before you go down that road, be compassionate and kind to yourself. Self-compassion can enhance your holistic well-being and people are drawn to those who get along with others easily," Sivaranjan continued.

"Eleanor Roosevelt said, *'No one can make you feel inferior without your consent.'* You should not take things personally, as other people's words and actions are the reflections of who they are, and the moment you take their words or actions to heart, you give them power over you," Sivaranjan elaborated.

"Always remember, you both, that you are on your unique journey and being happy for others' success comes from someone who practices a positive attitude. You should feel motivated and elated with their success, not jealous," Sivaranjan advised.

"Uncle, I could never have imagined a positive mental attitude goes to such lengths and breadths. I am starting my journey into the professional world, what will be a better way to embark on my journey with a positive mental attitude," Vaibhav said. "I am going to start practicing consistent optimism from now on. I know it will supercharge my performance and keep me on my heels at work."

"Dress up and show up because it is not the situation that challenges us, but our response to the situation," Sivaranjan emphasized.

"I am sure you both will maintain a positive attitude in life and at work for it will bring out the best in you," Sivaranjan assured him.

"This conversation has been truly enlightening, Uncle. I'm ready to embrace a consistent positive mental attitude," Vaibhav said with determination.

"That's the spirit, Vaibhav. Remember, a positive attitude is not about ignoring difficulties but about facing them with a mindset that helps you overcome them," Sivaranjan concluded with a smile.

Ananya spoke up. "I completely agree with everything we've discussed. A positive mental attitude is crucial not only in our professional lives but also in our personal lives. I've seen how a positive outlook can change the dynamic in group projects at college, making everyone more motivated and collaborative. I'm excited to apply this mindset in my career and see how it transforms my approach to challenges and opportunities."

"Absolutely, Ananya," Sivaranjan said. "Your positive attitude will be a powerful tool in navigating both personal and professional landscapes. Keep this optimism alive, and it will undoubtedly lead you to success."

"Thank you, Uncle," Ananya said with a smile. "This discussion has been a revelation in itself. I'm ready to face the world with a positive mental attitude."

"That's wonderful to hear, Ananya. Both of you have the potential to achieve great things with the right mindset. Embrace this positive attitude, and it will guide you through every challenge," Sivaranjan concluded warmly.

The Way Forward

———— ✦ ————

"Vaibhav and Ananya, while I have told you everything you should know about creating a successful transition, the real journey begins now," Sivaranjan began, his voice steady and earnest.

Sivaranjan leaned forward, his gaze intense. "Reflect on everything we have gone through together. Go through your notes, think about the key concepts, and consider how they apply to your own life. Internalizing these lessons will set you up for success."

"Reflection and internalization, got it," Vaibhav said, making a mental note. "I suppose setting clear goals is next?"

"Exactly," Sivaranjan affirmed. "Define both your short-term and long-term goals. Whether it's landing your first job, advancing in your career, or acquiring new skills, having clear, actionable goals will keep you focused and motivated."

"And then I need to create an action plan to achieve those goals," Vaibhav added thoughtfully.

"Right again," Sivaranjan said with a nod. "Break down your goals into manageable tasks with deadlines. This will give you direction and make your journey less overwhelming."

Ananya chimed in. "Continuous learning is key, isn't it, Uncle? Staying updated with industry trends, enrolling in relevant courses, and reading extensively?"

"Yes, Ananya," Sivaranjan replied. "Continuous learning will keep you competitive and adaptable in a rapidly changing job market."

"Building and maintaining professional relationships is also crucial," Ananya added. "Attending industry events, joining professional associations, and connecting with colleagues can open doors to new opportunities and provide valuable support throughout your career."

"And I must maintain a positive attitude," Vaibhav added, thinking back to the lessons on mindset.

"Absolutely," Sivaranjan said warmly. "Embrace challenges, stay resilient, and approach every situation with optimism. A positive attitude will enhance your work performance and improve your overall well-being."

"Developing soft skills is important too, right?" Vaibhav inquired.

"Yes," Sivaranjan affirmed. "Focus on communication, teamwork, and problem-solving. These skills are often as important as technical expertise and can significantly impact your career progression."

Ananya nodded. "And be prepared to adapt to new situations and challenges. The corporate world is dynamic, and the ability to pivot and embrace change will set you apart from your peers."

"Striving for a healthy work-life balance is also essential," Vaibhav said. "Dedication to your career is important, but ensuring you have time for relaxation, hobbies, and personal relationships is equally crucial for long-term success and happiness."

"Regular self-assessment is crucial too," Ananya added. "Periodically assessing your progress and adjusting your plans accordingly helps identify areas for improvement and celebrate achievements, keeping you motivated and on track."

"And we should give back to the community," Vaibhav said.

"Absolutely," Sivaranjan smiled. "As you grow in your career, find ways to give back. Whether through mentoring others, volunteering, or sharing your knowledge, contributing to your community can be highly rewarding and fulfilling."

Vaibhav looked thoughtful, "Uncle, this journey from campus to corporate seems like a big leap."

"It is," Sivaranjan agreed. "But remember, success isn't just about reaching the destination; it's about enjoying and learning from the journey. Stay curious, stay passionate, and most importantly, stay true to yourself. Your career is a canvas, and you have the tools and knowledge to create a masterpiece."

"Thank you, Uncle," Vaibhav said earnestly. "I feel ready to take on the world."

Ananya, equally moved, added, "Your guidance has been invaluable, Uncle. I'm excited to apply these lessons in my own journey."

Sivaranjan got a bit emotional and repeated himself, "Vaibhav, Ananya, as you both step into this new chapter of your lives, remember that it is just a new beginning," Sivaranjan began, his voice filled with warmth and pride. "You've learned a lot, but the real learning starts now. Embrace each moment with the same enthusiasm and curiosity you've shown throughout our conversations."

Vaibhav nodded, feeling a mix of excitement and gratitude. "I will, Uncle."

Ananya echoed, "Me too, Uncle. Your wisdom has given us a strong foundation."

Sivaranjan smiled, placing a hand on each of their shoulders. ***"Always stay true to yourselves, keep a positive attitude, and never stop striving for excellence.*** Life will present challenges, but I have no doubt that you will overcome them with grace and determination."

"Thank you, Uncle," Vaibhav replied, his eyes reflecting his sincerity.

"Remember, Vaibhav, Ananya, the journey ahead is filled with endless possibilities. Stay focused, be resilient, and cherish the lessons you learn along the way," Sivaranjan said, his voice carrying a hint of emotion. "I'm incredibly proud of you both, and I know you will achieve great things."

Vaibhav hugged his uncle tightly. "I won't let you down, Uncle. Thank you for everything."

Ananya wiped away a tear, her eyes shining with gratitude. "Thank you, Uncle. You've given us more than just lessons; you've shown us a vision for our future."

With a final nod and a heartfelt smile, Sivaranjan watched as Vaibhav and Ananya walked towards their futures, ready to embark on the new journeys that awaited them.

References

"What is Professionalism at Work?"https://harappa.education/ harappa-diaries/what-is-professionalism-at-work/. Harappa Education?Harappa-diaries. October 27, 2020.

Khamal, Bhupendra. "5 Myths of Professional Success." https:// yourstory.com/2014/03/professional-success-myth/amp, YourStory, March 21, 2014.

"Professionalism." https://career.vt.edu/develop/professionalism. html. Career and Professional Development. Virginia Tech.

Jacobs, Lacee. Quartarone, Mac. Hemingway, Kate. "Do Your Diversity Initiatives Promote Assimilation Over Inclusion?" https://hbr.org/2022/02/do-your-diversity-initiatives-promote-assimilation-over-inclusion?utm_campaign=hbr&utm_ medium=social&utm_source=facebook. Harvard Business Review, February 02, 2022

"9 Essential Communication Skills for any Workplace (and how to improve them)." VirtualSpeech, 15 February 2021, https:// virtualspeech.com/blog/communication-skills-in-the-workplace.

Barraclough, Dan. "Communication in the Workplace: Amazing Statistics." *Expert Market*, 9 March 2023, https://www.expertmarket.com/phone-systems/workplace-communication-statistics.

Doyle, Alison. "Communication Skills for Workplace Success." *The Balance*, 13 March 2021, https://www.thebalancemoney.com/communication-skills-list-2063779

"Communication - Importance of Good Communication Skills." *Corporate Finance Institute*, 13 March 2023, https://corporatefinanceinstitute.com/resources/careers/soft-skills/communication/.

"Effective Communication in Corporate World." *International Journal of Research and Analytical Reviews (IJRAR)*, http://ijrar.com/upload_issue/ijrar_issue_141.pdf.

Baldoni, John. "New Study: How Communication Drives Performance." *Harvard Business Review*, 19 November 2009, https://hbr.org/2009/11/new-study-how-communication-dr.

"Why Good Communication Skills Are Important for Your Career (with Tips to Develop Them)." *ProofHub*, https://www.proofhub.com/articles/good-communication-skills.

"Nonverbal Communication and Body Language." *HelpGuide.org*, 1 March 2023, https://www.helpguide.org/articles/relationships-communication/nonverbal-communication.htm.

"Body Language: An Effective Communication Tool." *Squarespace*, https://static1.squarespace.com/static/

56fb450bf8baf30bc33df806/t/58d1d7d7440243e31b951
3e8/1490147288845/Body+Language-+An+Effective+Com
munication+Tool.pdf.

"Body Language: Importance of Body Language in Communication." Harappa Education, 8 October 2020, https://harappa. education/harappa-diaries/body-language-in-communication/.

"Body Language - Beyond Words – How to Read Unspoken Signals." Mind Tools, https://www.mindtools.com/pages/ article/Body_Language.htm.

Coker, Diana, et al. "The Power of Power Dressing." The HR Digest, 25 April 2017, https://www.thehrdigest.com/power-power-dressing/.

"The Importance of Dressing Professionally at Work." Indeed, 10 March 2023, https://www.indeed.com/career-advice/starting-new-job/importance-dressing-professionally-at-work.

"What is power dressing and how to make it effective." Onmanorama, 23 September 2021, https://www.onmanorama. com/lifestyle/beauty-and-fashion/2021/09/23/power-dressing-effective.html.

"Home." YouTube, https://www.forbes.com/sites/ josephdeacetis/2020/08/22/the-importance-of-power-dressing-for-women-in-2020/?sh=43f3b0d66461.

Gore, Ira. "How To Dress-Up? Some Simple Power-Dressing Moves to Help You With Your Office Wardrobe." Fuzia, 25

February 2021, https://www.fuzia.com/blog/details/let-s-uncover-the-importance-of-power-dressing.

"7 Power Dressing Tips: What to Wear to Work?" Edarabia, https://www.edarabia.com/7-power-dressing-tips-what-wear-work/.

"How Power Dressing Will Help You Amplify Your Success." LinkedIn, 8 December 2020, https://www.linkedin.com/pulse/how-power-dressing-help-you-amplify-your-success-pradeep-agarwal.

Christie, Agatha. "Professionalism Quotes (178 quotes)." Goodreads, https://www.goodreads.com/quotes/tag/professionalism.

Tannen, Deborah. "The Power of Talk: Who Gets Heard and Why." Harvard Business Review, https://hbr.org/1995/09/the-power-of-talk-who-gets-heard-and-why.

Deeb, Carol. "Importance of Verbal Communication in Business." Bizfluent, 26 September 2017, https://bizfluent.com/info-7876762-importance-verbal-communication-business.html.

Bhasin, Hitesh. "Verbal Communication - Definition, Types, Importance and Difference from Non-Verbal." Marketing91, 18 October 2021, https://www.marketing91.com/verbal-communication/.

"Fluent Communication | Skills necessary for effective communication." Multibhashi, https://www.multibhashi.com/how-to-be-a-fluent-communicator/.

Baldoni, John. "Five Ways to Sharpen Your Communication Skills." Harvard Business Review, 30 April 2009, https://hbr.org/2009/04/five-things-leaders-can-do-to.

"Importance of Fluent Communication in Your Workspace: Let's Get Proficient in English Communication!" Fluent Life, 10 March 2022, https://thefluentlife.com/content/importance-fluent-communication-workspace-proficient-english/

"Choosing Your Words Wisely: Speaking the Language of Business Leadership." WSU Online MBA, 17 July 2020, https://onlinemba.wsu.edu/blog/choosing-your-words-wisely-speaking-the-language-of-business-leadership/

"Home." YouTube, https://writinghat.com/importance-of-articulation/.

"Why is Tone of Voice in Communication Important at Work?" SoundWave Global, 24 November 2021, https://www.soundwave.global/why-is-tone-of-voice-in-communication-important-at-work/

Birchard, Bill. "The Science of Strong Business Writing." Harvard Business Review, https://hbr.org/2021/07/the-science-of-strong-business-writing

"The 7 Cs of Communication." Professional Academy, https://www.professionalacademy.com/blogs/the-7-cs-of-communication/.

"Written Communication Quotes." QuotesGram, https://quotesgram.com/written-communication-quotes

"What a Compassionate Email Culture Looks Like." Harvard Business Review, 16 March 2021, https://hbr.org/2021/03/what-a-compassionate-email-culture-looks-like

"10 rules for email etiquette | The Law Society of NSW." Law Society, https://www.lawsociety.com.au/resources/resources/career-hub/10-rules-email-etiquette

O'Hara, Carolyn. "How to Improve Your Business Writing." Harvard Business Review, 20 November 2014, https://hbr.org/2014/11/how-to-improve-your-business-writing

Su, Jeff. "How to Write Better Emails at Work." Harvard Business Review, 30 August 2021, https://hbr.org/2021/08/how-to-write-better-emails-at-work

Dhawan, Erica. "Slow Down and Write Better Emails." Harvard Business Review, 19 February 2021, https://hbr.org/2021/02/slow-down-and-write-better-emails

"Written Communication | Inc.com." Inc. Magazine, https://www.inc.com/encyclopedia/written-communication.html

"Professionalism - Meeting the Standards That Matter." Mind Tools, https://www.mindtools.com/av44li2/professionalism

"[Professional Ethics] The Story of an Elderly Carpenter." LinkedIn, 12 September 2014, https://www.linkedin.com/pulse/20140912122335-81447169--professional-ethics-the-story-of-an-elderly-carpenter

"Understanding Workplace Values - How to Find People Who Fit Your Organization's Culture." Mind Tools, https://www.mindtools.com/ayjltrz/understanding-workplace-values

"The Importance of Values in the Workplace." SpriggHR, 27 February 2020, https://sprigghr.com/blog/hr-professionals/the-importance-of-values-in-the-workplace/

"Home." YouTube, https://andreiantoniu.com/moral-story-that-will-change-your-bad-habits/

"5 Benefits of Developing the Right Habits — Productive and Free." Productive and Free, 11 June 2018, https://www.productiveandfree.com/blog/benefits-of-habits

DePaul, Kristi. "What Does It Really Take to Build a New Habit?" Harvard Business Review, 2 February 2021, https://hbr.org/2021/02/what-does-it-really-take-to-build-a-new-habit

Rogers, Shalla. "How To Form (And Break) Habits In The Workplace." Insperity, https://www.insperity.com/blog/how-to-form-habits/

Schaninger, Bill, et al. "How organizations can build healthy employee habits." McKinsey, 6 July 2020, https://www.mckinsey.com/capabilities/people-and-organizational-performance/our-insights/the-organization-blog/how-organizations-can-build-healthy-employee-habits

Anzek, Fernanda. "How To Teach Employees Professionalism In The Workplace." Insperity, https://www.insperity.com/blog/professionalism-in-the-workplace

"Who is Elon Musk: Latest News on Elon Musk, Top News, Photos, Videos, Age." Business Standard, https://www.business-standard.com/about/who-is-elon-musk

Wallen, Daniel. "Success Habits of Elon Musk You Can Apply to Crush It in Your Life." PakWired, 7 January 2021, https://pakwired.com/success-habits-of-elon-musk-you-can-apply-to-crush-it-in-your-life/

Soots, Lynn. "What are Habits?" The Positive Psychology People, https://www.thepositivepsychologypeople.com/habits-to-happiness/

"11 Reasons Why Teamwork At The Office Is Important." Sling, https://getsling.com/blog/importance-of-teamwork/

Hansson, Heather. "The Importance of Teamwork in Your Organization." Docket, https://www.dockethq.com/resources/importance-of-teamwork-in-your-organization

Gent, Edd. "The unsurpassed 125-year-old network that feeds Mumbai." BBC, 14 January 2017, https://www.bbc.com/future/article/20170114-the-125-year-old-network-that-keeps-mumbai-going

Chaudhary, Arun Ray, et al. "Interpersonal Relationship at Workplace." All Things Talent, 8 April 2019, https://allthingstalent.org/interpersonal-relationship-at-workplace/

"Interpersonal Skills - Meaning, Importance, And Benefits Of Interpersonal Skills." Harappa Education, https://harappa.education/harappa-diaries/interpersonal-skills-all-you-need-to-know/

"Examples of interpersonal relationships (Interpersonal Traits)." *Zambianguardian*, 18 May 2022, https://www.zambianguardian.com/examples-of-interpersonal-relationships/

"Interpersonal Relationship at Workplace." *LinkedIn*, 18 November 2019, https://www.linkedin.com/pulse/interpersonal-relationship-workplace-sumista-banerjee

Singh, Anushruti, and Bhoomika Singh. "How HR leaders of Indian businesses handle workplace conflicts among employees." *SME Futures*, 13 July 2018, https://smefutures.com/hr-leaders-indian-businesses-handle-workplace-conflicts-among-employees/

"Resolving a Conflict at Workplace: Tips for Freshers." *Hyderabad India Online*, http://hyderabad-india-online.com/2012/05/resolving-conflict-workplace-freshers/

"Home." *YouTube*, https://www.forbes.com/sites/mikemyatt/2012/02/22/5-keys-to-dealing-with-workplace-conflict/?sh=6f4637001e95

Weitzman, Eben A., and Patricia Flynn. "Summary of "Problem Solving and Decision Making in Conflict Resolution." " *Beyond Intractability*, https://www.beyondintractability.org/artsum/weitzman-problem

"Conflict Management, Problem Solving and Decision Making." *TIGO Software Solutions*, https://tigosoftware.com/conflict-management-problem-solving-and-decision-making

Tahir, Junaid. "Children Playing Near Two Railway Tracks - Learn Something New !" *DailyTenMinutes*, http://www.

dailytenminutes.com/2018/12/children-playing-near-two-railway-tracks.html

"Decision—Making & Problem-Solving — BusinessBalls.com." BusinessBalls, https://www.businessballs.com/problem-solving-and-decision-making/decision-making-and-problem-solving/

"Decision-Making Style: A Guide to the 4 Types (With Examples)." Indeed, 10 March 2023, https://www.indeed.com/career-advice/career-development/decision-making-style

D'Silva, Donald. "STRONG POSITIVE ATTITUDE AMONG SUCCESSFUL PERSONALITIES." Mangalorean.com, 14 June 2021, https://www.mangalorean.com/strong-positive-attitude-among-successful-personalities/

"On This Day In 1989: A 16-Year-Old Sachin Tendulkar Became The Youngest Player To Score A Test Fifty | Cricket News." NDTV Sports, https://sports.ndtv.com/cricket/on-this-day-in-1989-a-16-year-old-sachin-tendulkar-became-the-youngest-player-to-score-a-test-fifty-2622586

"Famous People Who Succeeded Due To Affirmations and Positive Mindset." ThinkUp, 6 November 2017, https://thinkup.me/positive-mindset-affirmations/

Eatough, Erin. "How to Cultivate a Positive Mental Attitude for Success." BetterUp, 8 November 2021, https://www.betterup.com/blog/positive-mental-attitude

"Small Wins A Reason to Celebrate - Jammu Kashmir Latest News | Tourism | Breaking News J&K." Daily Excelsior,

27 March 2022, https://www.dailyexcelsior.com/small-wins-a-reason-to-celebrate/

"The 10 secret mindsets of Indian business success." LinkedIn, 3 April 2016, https://www.linkedin.com/pulse/10-secret-mindsets-indian-business-success-stephen-manallack

"My courage is my capital: Chetna Gala Sinha." The Indian Express, 3 August 2020, https://indianexpress.com/article/lifestyle/life-positive/my-courage-is-my-capital-chetna-gala-sinha-6536077/

"10 Indians who succeeded against all odds." IndiaFilings, 21 April 2014, https://www.indiafilings.com/learn/10-indians-who-succeeded-against-all-odds/

Carter, Peter. "7 Ways How Smart Leaders Have the Ability to Read People." 101Productivity, 3 February 2020, https://101productivity.com/ways-how-smart-leader-read-people/

"Home." YouTube, https://www.businessinsider.in/strategy/how-to-become-a-mind-reader-to-get-ahead-in-your-career/articleshow/48717180.cms.

Paler, Jude, et al. "How to read people like a pro: 17 tricks from psychology." Hack Spirit, https://hackspirit.com/how-to-read-people/

"What Should You Know About Reading People?" BetterHelp, 11 January 2023, https://www.betterhelp.com/advice/general/what-should-you-know-about-reading-people/

"Home." YouTube, https://assets-global.website-files.com/5f3ae94489e0968a6114dc24/61eead9090c02ce556ebc8

"Your speech pace: guide to speeding and slowing down." SpeakerHub, 22 January 2017, https://speakerhubhq.medium.com/your-speech-pace-guide-to-speeding-and-slowing-down-be150dcb9cd7

Gudisa, Srujan. "Communication tips: How to harness the power of pause." The Enterprisers Project, 15 September 2020, https://enterprisersproject.com/article/2020/9/communication-tips-how-harness-power-pause

"Home." YouTube, https://media-exp1.licdn.com/dms/image/C5112AQE33AoUhKfIYQ/article-cover_image-shrink_600_2000/0/1553332780685?e=2147483647&v=beta&t=Z3KY6RovsrUS8D1iOL1do9NOmxQ59hvwYy8tcm7yaXo

"Ray Tomlinson | Lemelson." Lemelson-MIT, https://lemelson.mit.edu/resources/ray-tomlinson

"Home." YouTube, https://www.forbes.com/sites/forbesbusinessdevelopmentcouncil/2020/02/13/how-mastering-teamwork-will-make-your-organization-successful/?sh=562700f43f08

"Teamwork —Together Everyone Achieves More." The Hans India, 17 June 2016, https://www.thehansindia.com/posts/index/Hans/2016-06-16/Teamwork-Together-Everyone-Achieves-More/235672

"The Importance of Interpersonal Relationships for Your Health." AdventHealth, 3 December 2018, https://www.adventhealth.com/hospital/adventhealth-gordon/news/importance-interpersonal-relationships-your-health

10 Examples Of Unconscious Bias In The Workplace And How to Avoid Them.

EasyLlama, https://www.easyllama.com/blog/unconscious-bias-in-the-workplace.

Women in leadership: What's the holdup?" S&P Global, 7 March 2024, https://www.spglobal.com/esg/insights/featured/special-editorial/women-in-leadership-what-s-the-holdup.

Wong, Kellie. "Benefits and Challenges of Diversity & Inclusion in the Workplace." Achievers, 25 March 2024, https://www.achievers.com/blog/diversity-and-inclusion/.

About the Author

Life is very interesting, some of our greatest pains become our greatest strengths." Dr. Jimmy Jain embodies this truth, with his unwavering commitment to making a difference, and his extraordinary success in life and business reflects his resilience and determination. On one of his business travel, while he was running in Mysore, Dr. Jimmy was hit by a drunk biker, suffering a head injury that required stitches. Despite this setback, with a training session scheduled for the following morning, Jimmy's determination to deliver remained unshaken. Recognizing the power of the mind, he aimed to exemplify the concept of "Mind over Matter." With meticulous precautions and the unwavering support of his team, he stood ready to lead the session just 13 hours after the accident, showcasing his resilience and optimism.

Dr. Jimmy's experience corroborates the power of perseverance and belief, inspiring others to embrace their inner strength and maintain a positive mindset. He encourages everyone to believe that with the right mindset, dreams can indeed come true.

Recipient of the Outstanding Leadership Award and the Bhartiya Gyan Ratna Award for "Outstanding Life and Business Coach" and featured in the Top 100 Global Thought Leaders to Inspire You in 2021 by the People Hum Leadership Series, Dr. Jimmy is a prominent figure in leadership and personal development. A member of the Forbes Coaches Council, his insights and expertise are regularly featured on Forbes.com.

He holds a Doctor of Philosophy in Innovation and Design Thinking, has studied Neuroscience and Leadership at Harvard, earned his Master's degree from the Indian Institute of Management Kozhikode, and holds a Diploma in Instrument Technology from the Indo-Swiss Training Centre. He is a Certified Leadership Circle Coach, a Gallup Coach specializing in Clifton

StrengthsFinder & Builder Profile 10, and the author of five influential books, including "Design Thinking for Start-ups," "Train The Trainer," "Design Thinking Playbook," "Designing Exceptionally Amazing Life," and "The Alchemy of Mentorship."

As the Visionary Founder of "SEQUEL" and the "Society of Design Thinking Professionals," Dr. Jimmy is also a Founding Member of the Leadership Excellence India Chapter at Harvard Square, Boston, USA. He is a Subject Matter Expert in Net Promoter Score and the Lost Dutchman Gold Mine simulation. With nearly 24 years of diverse experience, spanning a decade in Manufacturing, Strategic Sourcing, Sales, and Marketing, followed by over 14 years as an entrepreneur in building people capabilities and consulting across various industries, Dr. Jimmy has significantly impacted companies at every stage of their maturity, from start-ups to established multinationals.

Afreen Fatima

Editor of the Book

Invite Dr. Jimmy to Speak

Book Dr. Jimmy Jain to speak at your event and he is guaranteed to deliver an incredibly INSPIRING, and truly LIFE-CHANGING experience for everyone in attendance!

For more than two decades, Dr. Jimmy Jain has been consistently rated as a top keynote speaker by the top firms in India. His unique style combines inspiring audiences with his remarkable TRUE story, keeping them engaged with his high-energy, and empowering them with actionable strategies to elevate their RESULTS to the next level.

Testimonials:

Dr. Jimmy Jain's session at Konsociate on 3rd August was nothing short of extraordinary. As an eminent industry leader and one of the Top 100 Global Thought Leaders, he inspired us with his insights on smart goal setting and the relentless pursuit of excellence. Jimmy's mentorship promises to transform our EPGP journey, turning knowledge into real-life success. Together, we can move mountains.

– Konsociate

Jimmy is known for transitioning from one role to another. He has spotted white spaces and taken risks by making his and others' journeys unique.

– Tractors and Farm Equipment Ltd

Jimmy is the most enigmatic trainer and facilitator one could ask for. He doesn't just ensure that the learning outcomes are achieved however ensures value is delivered. He is a lifelong coach and mentor to all those who get the opportunity to associate with him. Knowing him means signing up for an ongoing learning and growth program and I am fortunate enough to have had that opportunity. His strong belief is to learn, unlearn and relearn and while working with his clients he embodies that in his consultative approach, bringing on board unique yet personalised curated solutions. It has been a pleasure knowing, learning and growing with him.

– Australian Network on Disability

Jimmy has all qualities of being a great guide. He is smart, quick, sharp and willing to co-operate. Has taken decisions which are difficult for most and his success is an example in itself.

– Rajan Chugh, DGM – Sales India2

ŠKODA AUTO Volkswagen India Private Limited

Jimmy is a fantastic coach and having total grip on the subject. His insight on Design Thinking have open my eyes to look beyond imagination. Had a great time with him. I wish him to continue such programmes and add more Design thinkers.

– Anil Santwani, Head of Operations

Yes Bank

Sevan Startup Summit 2019 created an opportunity to attend Jimmy's workshop in design thinking, where I learnt the circles of design thinking and had fun while preparing prototypes of imaginative products! Jimmy's workshops are super interactive, engaging and fun! I use some of the learnings shared by Jimmy when I, as a trainer run workshops in community based tourism product design.

– Arpi Umedyan, Talent Business Partner

Ucom

I met Jimmy at Seaside Startup Summit and was immediately impressed by his willingness to support and guide new startup founders like myself. He is a very inspirational mentor and not a single moment spent with him goes to waste.

– Nver Kassis, Founder and CEO

Agency Cloud9

Excellent communicator and has amazing influence over people. He has the ability to grow on you, especially during his training sessions. He is an expert in his domain and can put together the most precise training solution for any kind of need. He is great person to work with and I would definitely recommend his services.

– Roopa Khatri, Talent Acquisition and

Employee Experience

TotalEnergies

Jimmy is one of the few Business Partners, who not only delves deep into the requirement but also relates extremely well to the business of the company. He is full of energy and has the ability to hold a large and highly intellectual crowd together for a relatively long period. Is very creative and comes up with impromptu activities to keep people engaged and lives up to his reputation of being result oriented. Good Team worker and flexible to adverse conditions.

All in All.... a package you just can't ignore and therefore have engaged him and his team in on various occasions over the last few years.

–Nihal Kotal, Founder and Director

Peoplenomic Consulting Pvt. Ltd.

I have known Jimmy Jain since the Mahindra & Mahindra days. He is an absolute powerhouse with unending energy and vibrance. I find him to be very innovative too. He has the ability to create new market areas through clear thinking and hard work. He also has a very strong ability to develop consensus with his thinking process within a group. His entrepreneurial quality stands out. Overall I believe that Jimmy is a very thorough professional with a strong acumen and is a wonderful person to work with, as a colleague or as a business partner.

– Maharaj Mukherjee

Lexus India

I have had the distinct pleasure of knowing Jimmy Jain. I found Jimmy to be consistently pleasant coach, facilitating the trainings with dedication and a smile. He has been more than the ideal trainer. Besides being a joy to work with, Jimmy is a take-charge person who is able to present creative ideas and communicate the benefits. He has his own unique way of mentoring, guiding and executing the trainings. He will make sure that you LEARN and APPLY the learning's in your day today business proceedings.

– Sameer Borse, Business Director and Designated Partner – South Asia

Agnus Chemical Company

Jimmy Jain has done a remarkable job in facilitating our change management process here at Lubrizol India. His high energy positive style permeated the meetings and his skill in getting people to open up allowed free flow of ideas. Finally and most importantly he emphasized and facilitated the plan forward. Definitely he is a very skilled facilitator and trainer.

–Timothy Earl Madden, Founder and CEO

LiNK-BT

Jimmy comes across as a People's Person and hence his professional area of work best suits him. Extremely amiable and easily builds rapport with people around, from the bottom to the top of the hierarchy. His knowledge and understanding of the subject is immense, which works wonder as then the so called uninteresting-training-sessions turn out to be involving, exciting and out-of-the-ordinary learning sessions.

– Supriya Jain, HR Leader

VIP Industries Ltd.

Jimmy is a very jovial, responsible and energetic person. He is a person with very high integrity and discipline. He is able to manage and maintain good relations with all. He is a good trainer and brings in a lot of freshness and innovation in his training sessions.

– Vinod Nair, Head – Human Resource

Mahindra Finance

For more information, write to him at jimmy@jimmyjain.com

Other Books by the Author